The Way to the Eternal Purpose of God

The Way to the Eternal Purpose of God

Lance Lambert

LANCE LAMBERT MINISTRIES

Richmond, Virginia, USA

Copyright © 2019
Lance Lambert Ministries
Richmond, VA
USA
All rights reserved

ISBN: 978-1-68389-101-7

www.lancelambert.org

Contents

Preface 7
1. The Heart of God from the Beginning 9
2. Baptism, Transfiguration, Gethsemane 23
3. Yes, Even the Death of the Cross 39
4. Love Not the World 55
5. What is Worldliness? 69
6. A Living Sacrifice 85

*Unless otherwise indicated, Scripture quotations
are from the American Standard Version 1901*

Preface

Lance has shared many messages on "The Eternal Purpose of God," but in these messages he reveals "The Way to the Eternal Purpose of God." These messages were given at the West Coast Christian Conference in 2005 and 2006. The first three speak to us on "The Cross and the Christ." In them Lance shares on the life of Christ from His birth, to His baptism and the anointing of the Spirit for the three and a half years of His ministry, to His transfiguration, to the garden of Gethsemane and finally to the cross. This is the way that our Lord lived and walked in the form of a Man here on earth, and He has called each one of His blood-bought ones to follow Him by His indwelling life that entered in at the time of a new birth.

The second three messages are concerning "The Cross and the World." Lance asks these questions: "What is worldliness? What is the greatest destroyer of the church? Do you know the character of this world?" He answers these questions in a way that leaves no doubt that there is only one way to overcome the world and that is through the cross. We see in the life of the Lord Jesus what it means to be a living sacrifice (Romans 12:1), and this is the calling upon all of His people. So the challenge to worldliness is submitting and obedience to the Lordship of Christ. Then we can simply say as Mary did: "Whatsoever He says, do it."

1. The Heart of God from the Beginning

Revelation 13:8
And all that dwell on the earth shall worship him (the antichrist), every one whose name hath not been written from the foundation of the world in the book of life of the Lamb that hath been slain.

Philippians 2:5–11
Have this mind in you, which was also in Christ Jesus: who, existing in the form of God, counted not the being on an equality with God a thing to be grasped, but emptied himself, taking the form of a servant, being made in the likeness of men; and being found in fashion as a man, he humbled himself, becoming obedient even unto death, yea, the death of the cross. Wherefore also God highly exalted him and gave unto him the name which is above every name; that at the name of Jesus every knee should bow, of things in heaven and things on earth and things under the earth, and that every tongue should confess

that Jesus Christ is Lord, to the glory of God the Father.

Hebrews 5:7–10
Who in the days of his flesh, having offered up prayers and supplications with strong crying and tears unto him that was able to save him from death, and having been heard for his godly fear, though he was a Son, yet learned obedience by the things which he suffered; and having been made perfect, he became unto all them that obey him the author of eternal salvation; named of God a high priest after the order of Melchizedek.

Shall we pray:

Beloved Lord, we are so thankful we are found here in Your presence, and we praise You, Lord, that You have made specific provision for us all. Many of us have travelled long journeys to come here, and we are tired. Beloved Lord, You have made a provision of renewing spirit, soul, and body, and into that renewing power and grace of Yours we stand by faith. Would You ban all tiredness and revive us that we may be able to attend to You? We thank You, Lord, that You have made a provision for the speaking of Your Word, the translating, and the hearing. We thank You for that anointing grace and power that You have made available to us, and into that anointing we stand by faith. Make this a time when You meet with us, Lord, when You write indelibly on our hearts that which is eternal and cannot be taken away. Do it, oh Lord. Even at the very beginning of our conference, come in with all the power of Your presence, and we ask this in the name of our Messiah, the Lord Jesus. Amen.

The theme of this conference is: *The Way to the Eternal Purpose of God—The Cross.* For the Lord Jesus there was no other way to the fulfilment of God's eternal purpose but the cross. There was no alternative. The only way that God could save mankind was through the cross. The only way the purpose of God could be fulfilled for the creation, for the universe, for mankind was through Calvary, so I would like to look firstly at the cross in the heart of God from the foundation of the world. Secondly, I would like to look at Bethlehem, the birth of a Babe—the Word became flesh and dwelt among us. Thirdly, I want to look at the thirty-three years of the earthly life of our Lord Jesus.

The Cross in the Heart of God

Revelation 13:8 speaks of everyone whose name has not been written from the foundation of the world in the book of life of the Lamb that has been slain. There are two ways that we can translate the Greek. You will notice in your margin that you will have an alternative rendering, at least in the good Bible study versions, in two ways. One is: "Everyone whose name is not written in the book of life of the Lamb that has been slain from the foundation of the world." The other rendering is: "Everyone whose name has not been written from the foundation of the world in the book of life of the Lamb that has been slain." It does not matter how you render the Greek, it means the same. No single name of a human being can be written in the Lamb's book of life without the cross.

Your name was written in the Lamb's book of life because of Calvary, not because of your goodness or your devotion. It was not because your parents or your grandparents are Christians or because of another relative who is a Christian. That is not the reason you are in the Lamb's book of life. You are in the Lamb's book of life because of Calvary and because the Spirit of God made the Lamb of God, who bore away the sin of the world, a reality to you. So whether we translate this; "Everyone whose name is in the Lamb's book of life who was slain from the foundation of the world," or whether we put it the other way, the fact of the matter is that the cross was in the heart of God from the beginning.

God did not create this whole world and mankind, Adam and Eve, and then Adam and Eve made the wrong choice. God did not, if I may put it irrelevantly, scratch His head and say, "Oh, dear, dear, dear, they have made the wrong choice, what can I do?" and then thought of the cross. No! When God created man, He knew precisely what was going to happen, and Calvary was in His heart from the beginning. That is why He went on with it. That is why when Adam and Eve fell, He still went on with His purpose.

The principle of the cross is in the very character of the Godhead. There is no arrogance in the Godhead, no grasping for power, no fighting for position. The principle of the cross was in the very heart and mind of the Godhead from the beginning. Calvary is the supreme expression of the heart and mind of God. It is the way that God can most perfectly and completely be understood. God had to give His Son; His Son had to come. It is not that somehow the cross was an afterthought, but because of the kind of Person God is, Calvary was a necessity; therefore we have this wonderful phrase: "The Lamb slain from the foundation of the world."

Psalm 40:6–8 says,

"Sacrifice and offering thou hast no delight in; mine ears hast thou opened: Burnt-offering and sin-offering hast thou not required. Then said I, Lo, I am come; in the roll of the book it is written of me: I delight to do thy will, O my God; yea, thy law is within my heart."

This is an amazing messianic prophecy, speaking of the Lord Jesus. Somewhere in times eternal before ever the world was created, God said, "Who will go for Us? Who will give Himself for the salvation of this world?" Jesus said, "Lo, I am come to do thy will O God." It says, "Sacrifice and burnt offering thou hast no delight in." But when the Lord Jesus said, "I delight to do thy will O God," it was Calvary. When He said, "Your law is written on My heart," it meant the death of the cross. There was no other way.

"For it is impossible that the blood of bulls and goats should take away sins. Wherefore when he cometh into the world, he saith, Sacrifice and offering thou wouldest not, but a body didst thou prepare for me; in whole burnt offerings and sacrifices for sin thou hadst no pleasure: Then said I, Lo, I am come (In the roll of the book it is written of me) to do thy will, O God. Saying above, Sacrifices and offerings and whole burnt offerings and sacrifices for sin thou wouldest not, neither hadst pleasure therein (that which are offered according to the law), then hath he said, Lo, I am come to do thy will. He

> *taketh away the first that he may establish the second. By which will we have been sanctified through the offering of the body of Jesus Christ once for all. And every priest indeed standeth day by day ministering and offering oftentimes the same sacrifices, that which can never take away sins: but he, when he had offered one sacrifice for sins for ever, sat down on the right hand of God; henceforth expecting till his enemies be made the footstool of his feet." (Hebrews 10:4–13)*

The blood of bulls and goats cannot take away sin. The Spirit of God interprets that amazing messianic prophecy in Psalm 40, that when Jesus had offered one sacrifice for sins forever He sat down on the right hand of God. That meant when the Lord Jesus said, "Here am I, send Me," it was your salvation and my salvation that was wrought. All those wonderful sacrifices were but a picture of something far more tremendous and wonderful. They all pointed to the sacrifice of the Lord Jesus once for all times. It says, "By which will we have been sanctified to the offering of the body of Jesus Christ once for all" (v. 10). Calvary was not an afterthought of God. Calvary was not a kind of action on the part of God to restore damage after it had happened. It was in the heart of God from the beginning. He founded a foundation, a basis upon which He could deal with sinful mankind and a fallen universe.

> *In the beginning was the Word, and the Word was with God, and the Word was God. The same was in the beginning with God. All things were made through him; and without him was not anything made that hath been made ... And the Word became flesh and dwelt among us (and we beheld his glory,*

glory as of the only begotten from the Father), full of grace and truth ... For the law was given through Moses; grace and truth came through Jesus Christ. No man hath seen God at any time; the only begotten Son, who is in the bosom of the Father, He hath declared him. (John 1:1–3, 14, 17–18)

The Word Became Flesh

So the Word became flesh and dwelt among us. And in the same chapter John says, "Behold, the Lamb of God who beareth away the sin of the world!" (v. 29). It is to me something tremendous just to think for a few moments together that the cross was in the heart of the Godhead from the very beginning. It is the very expression of the character and heart of God.

Secondly is Bethlehem, and it is all, of course, bound together. Can you believe that God Himself came into this world, conceived by the Holy Spirit in the womb of a woman? It is beyond us. Think! "The Word became flesh." "In the beginning was the Word." That is the intelligence, the mind. I like to put it as the heart and mind of God. It is the intelligence articulated. (You who are Caucasian American background say, "verbalized.") But that is the word. If I stood here and said nothing, you would just have to imagine what I was thinking. But these words are the articulation of the mind and the heart of God.

"In the beginning was the Word, and the Word was with God, and the Word was God, and the Word became flesh and dwelt among us." Here is the cross in action before Calvary became a fact. That little Baby cradled in the arms of a woman was the Word of God; He was God. It baffles us. You mean that God the Son put

Himself in a position of limitation, of restriction, of dependence, that He was dependent on His mother for food? It is amazing! It is the principle of the cross before Calvary ever became a historic fact. There in the arms of Mary was the Word of God—so small, so seemingly weak, so subject to restriction.

> *Philippians 2:5–8a: "Have this mind in you, which was also in the Messiah Jesus: who, existing in the form of God, counted not the being on an equality with God a thing to be grasped, but emptied himself, taking the form of a bond slave, being made in the likeness of men; and being found in fashion as a man, he humbled himself."*

Amazing! Before Calvary ever took place, we see Calvary in Bethlehem. He was born to die. The very meaning of His coming into this world was to die. For there was no other way for the fulfilment of God's eternal purpose. He took this unbelievable step of putting Himself into a position of weakness. A bond slave is the lowest form of service, one who is owned by another with no rights. Can you believe this! This is your Saviour. This is the Lover of your soul. No one else has ever loved you like this—neither husband nor wife nor father nor mother, nor children. No one has ever loved you like this. In order to fulfil God's eternal purpose and to bring many sons to glory, He reduced Himself to one foot of flesh. He was born of a woman, cradled in the arms of a human being, and He did this for you.

> *"And being found in fashion as a man, he humbled himself, becoming obedient even unto death, yea,*

the death of the cross" (Philippians 2:8).

You have this same thought in the second letter of the apostle Paul to the Corinthians:

"For ye know the grace of our Lord Jesus the Messiah, that, though he was rich, yet for your sakes he became poor, that ye through his poverty might become rich" (II Corinthians 8:9).

"For ye know the grace of our Lord Jesus." Do you? Has the grace of our Lord Jesus ever dawned on you? There was no other way to save you. He did this that you might be introduced to the unsearchable riches that are His, that you might become a joint-heir with Him. Oh, the grace of our Lord Jesus! "You know the grace of our Lord Jesus that though He was rich, yet He became poor." This is the principle of the cross. Before ever Calvary became a fact, there you see it in action. He was rich, on an equality with God, yet He became poor, that you might become rich—the cross and the Christ.

Have This Mind in You

Isn't it interesting that it says in Philippians, "Have this mind in you"? Some of the new versions say, "Have this attitude." Have this mind, the same mind. It is also interesting that it is in the plural, "Have this mind among you." All our problems in the work of the Lord, all our problems in the churches go back to this thing, that we do not have the mind of the Lord Jesus. Rather it is I, I—I think, I feel, I want, I see. I, I, and I. If you have I, I, and I, you have trouble, and that is what happens in nearly every assembly of God's people.

It is the exact opposite to having the mind of the Messiah Jesus. The mind of the Lord Jesus was not I, but the Father, to become a bond slave, to have no rights, to serve others. That was the mind of the Lord Jesus.

Many of us would prefer to be hired servants. You have definite hours. You start at nine and end at five. You have rights, you have wages, and a whole lot of other things. Most of our churches are made up of servants, not bond slaves. "Oh, of course we are serving the Lord—from nine to five." We are serving the Lord on certain terms. "Have this mind among you."

Two thirds, no, three quarters of the conflicts in our assemblies would be settled by having the mind of Christ. If we said, "I am going to be a bond slave of the Lord Jesus," it would settle everything. What kind of mind do you have? "Oh," you say, "I am saved." I am glad to hear it. "I am born again." I am glad to hear it. What are the terms on which you are serving the Lord? When the Lord saved you, He meant for you to become like Him, to have the same mind, the same attitude. It is tremendous—the cross and the Messiah.

If the Lord Jesus appeared to many of us, we would hardly recognize Him. I think that the church in Laodicea was so interesting. They were all born-again people. It was a New Testament church—not denominational, not traditional, not institutional. They had the Lord's table, maybe once a week or every day, we do not know. They had regular Bible studies, prayer meetings, evangelistic outreaches. They had everything and they themselves felt they had everything. "Of course, we have everything in Christ. We see; those others do not even see. We know; we have faith. We are clothed and on our way to glory." But the Lord Jesus, the Head of the church and the Saviour of the body was outside of the whole assembly, and He was knocking. It is the most plaintive voice, with the most plaintive words that Jesus ever spoke: "If any man hear My voice ..." They were studying His Word, they were studying His life, they were studying the truth that was in Him. They were singing hymns and songs about Him. They were breaking bread to remember Him, and He was outside knocking on the door and saying, "Is there anyone who can hear Me?" Can you believe it? "Have this mind in you." Apparently, from the leadership to the simplest saint in Laodicea, nobody had the mind of the Lord Jesus. Do you know how He described them? Poor—they thought they were rich; they were wretched, blind, and naked—what a catalogue! These are believers, but they did not have the mind of the Lord Jesus.

The Son Learned Obedience

"Though he was a Son, yet learned obedience by the things which he suffered; and having been made perfect, he became unto all them that obey him the author of eternal salvation." (Hebrews 5:8–9)

These are mysterious words. "Though He was a Son, He yet learned obedience by the things which he suffered; and having been made complete (I like that better than perfect because the idea of perfection is that He had sin, and we know He had no sin.), having been made mature, having come to maturity." Even the

Lord Jesus, without sin, was made complete and mature through the things which He suffered.

What were the things that He suffered? Maybe it is just as well we do not know. But what were the things that He suffered? Hebrews 12:3 tells us that "He endured the contradiction of sinners," "the gainsaying of sinners" is another English word for it. What did that mean? Did it mean that when as a carpenter He made something out of wood and someone told Him it was not good enough? How did He react? We believe, by the way, that this word *carpenter* is probably better in Hebrew as *kablan* which means "a contractor." He worked both in iron, stone, and wood. We do not know the things He suffered, but I am quite sure that in those twenty or more years that He worked as a *kablan* there must have been many contradictions of sinners. We know He began His messianic ministry when He was thirty years of age. We know that the reference in Hebrews 5:7 is to Gethsemane: "Who in the days of his flesh, having offered up prayers and supplications with strong crying and tears unto him that was able to save him from death, and having been heard for his godly fear, though he was a Son, yet learned obedience by the things which he suffered." Not as I will, but as Thou will.

Here is something tremendous. This principle of the cross has been in the heart and mind of God from the beginning. It has never *not* been there. Calvary is the very expression of the kind of Person God is—Father, Son, and Holy Spirit.

May the Lord help us. We know so many limitations, so many difficult circumstances, so many things that depress us, hem us in, put us in a strait jacket. The Lord Jesus knew all about this, and He who lives in you has already gone through all of this and overcome. "Though He was a Son, yet learned He obedience through the things which He suffered." There is nothing that God is asking of you that the Lord Jesus has not gone through and overcome, and in you He can be the Overcomer.

Let us pray:

Beloved Lord, we want to thank You for Your grace, that though You were so rich, You became poor that through Your poverty we might become rich. Beloved Lord, open our eyes. Help us to see the Lord Jesus in a new way. Touch the eyes of our hearts, and if nothing else, renew the first love that was once in our hearts. Help us to fall in love with You. Lord, do it for Your name sake. Amen.

2.
Baptism, Transfiguration, Gethsemane

Matthew 3:13–17
Then cometh Jesus from Galilee to the Jordan unto John, to be baptized of him. But John would have hindered him, saying, I have need to be baptized of thee, and comest thou to me? But Jesus answering said unto him, Suffer it now: for thus it becometh us to fulfil all righteousness. Then he suffereth him. And Jesus, when he was baptized, went up straightway from the water: and lo, the heavens were opened unto him, and he saw the Spirit of God descending as a dove, and coming upon him; and lo, a voice out of the heavens, saying, This is my beloved Son, in whom I am well pleased.

Matthew 17:1–8
And after six days Jesus taketh with him Peter, and James, and John his brother, and bringeth them up into a high mountain apart: and he was transfigured before them; and his face did shine as the sun, and his garments became white as the light. And behold, there

appeared unto them Moses and Elijah talking with him. And Peter answered, and said unto Jesus, Lord, it is good for us to be here: if thou wilt, I will make here three tabernacles; one for thee, and one for Moses, and one for Elijah. While he was yet speaking, behold, a bright cloud overshadowed them: and behold, a voice out of the cloud, saying, This is my beloved Son, in whom I am well pleased; hear ye him. And when the disciples heard it, they fell on their face, and were sore afraid. And Jesus came and touched them and said, Arise, and be not afraid. And lifting up their eyes, they saw no one, save Jesus only.

Matthew 26:36–45

Then cometh Jesus with them unto a place called Gethsemane, and saith unto his disciples, Sit ye here, while I go yonder and pray. And he took with him Peter and the two sons of Zebedee, and began to be sorrowful and sore troubled. Then saith he unto them, My soul is exceeding sorrowful, even unto death: abide ye here, and watch with me. And he went forward a little, and fell on his face, and prayed, saying, My Father, if it be possible, let this cup pass away from me: nevertheless, not as I will, but as thou wilt. And he cometh unto the disciples, and findeth them sleeping, and saith unto Peter, What, could ye not watch with me one hour? Watch and pray, that ye enter not into temptation: the spirit indeed is willing, but the flesh is weak. Again a second time he went away, and prayed, saying, My Father, if this cannot pass away, except I drink it, thy will be done. And he came again and found them sleeping, for their eyes were heavy. And he left them again, and went away, and prayed a third time, saying again the same words. Then cometh he to the disciples, and saith unto them, Sleep on now, and take your rest: behold, the hour is at hand, and the Son of man is betrayed into the hands of sinners.

Luke 22:43–44
And there appeared unto him (Jesus) an angel from heaven, strengthening him. And being in an agony he prayed more earnestly; and his sweat became as it were great drops of blood falling down upon the ground.

Shall we pray:

Beloved Lord, we are so thankful that we are found here in Your presence. We need You, Lord. We need You for the speaking, the translating, and the hearing. I can outline truths, my brother can translate them, and we can hear truths, but unless You are here present as the power and grace in the speaking, translating, and hearing, nothing will go through into eternity. We are living at such a dangerous point in the history of the world, and in many ways a turning point in the history of the church. Beloved Lord, meet with us. To that end we stand by faith into the anointing that You have provided through the finished work of our Lord Jesus. Into that anointing grace and power we stand by faith. Let the speaking be anointed, the translating be anointed, and the hearing be anointed; then Lord, we believe that Your purpose in our time together will be fulfilled. Hear this our prayer, for we ask it in the name of the Messiah our Lord Jesus. Amen.

The Baptism of the Christ

I spoke of three matters concerning "The Cross and the Christ." The first was the fact that from the very foundation of the world the cross was in the heart of God. Before even the world was created the Lord Jesus had said, "I am ready to go." Then we spoke about Bethlehem, when God the Son became flesh, when He became just a foot of flesh and blood, dependent upon a woman, accepting restriction, limitation—the things that we all feel at times. It was the cross in action. Jesus was born to die; that was the reason for His birth. It was that He might come thirty-three years later to Calvary and die in our place in order that He might save us and bring us back to God's eternal purpose. Lastly I spoke about the thirty-three years of the life of our Lord Jesus: "Though He was a Son, yet learned He obedience by the things which He suffered, and being made complete or mature, He became the author of eternal salvation." We do not know all the many things that the Lord Jesus had to suffer—the contradiction of people, the gainsaying of people, those who argued with Him, those who told Him when He was young that He was wrong, those who returned His work to Him and said there were flaws in it when there were no flaws. We do not know what the Lord Jesus suffered, but through it all He learned obedience, and that is the cross in action.

I want to take three more events in the life of our Lord Jesus—the baptism of the Christ, the transfiguration of the Christ, and the victory won by the Christ. The first, of course, is the baptism of Jesus which we read in Matthew chapter 3. Why did the Lord Jesus get baptised? If it was the baptism of John the Baptist, it was the baptism of repentance. But Jesus did not need to repent.

Though He was tempted in all points like as we are, He was without sin. Why then did He come to John and ask him to baptise Him? He was not a sinner; He had no sins to wash away. What exactly was it? Was it for religious reasons? We have in the Jewish religion to this day what is called the "mikveh." Jews can be baptised many times. As soon as you are defiled or when you touch something dead, you have to be baptised. Was it for that reason Jesus was baptised? No, I do not think so.

John said, "Why do You come to me to baptise You? I need to be baptised by You." But the Lord Jesus said, "Suffer it now that I might fulfil all righteousness." I think the New American Standard Bible is better in its rendering in English: "Permit it at this time; for in this way it is fitting for us to fulfil all righteousness." Those waters of baptism spoke of death just as they speak of death for you and me. When the Lord Jesus went down into those waters of baptism, He was confirming in the sight of the Father why He had come into the world. It was not just to work miracles, although that was part of it. It was not just to teach the revelation of the heart and mind of God. It was to die, and at thirty years of age the Lord Jesus committed Himself to the death of the cross three years before it happened.

The Heavens Opened

The moment Jesus stepped into those waters and committed Himself to the death of the cross, something happened that had never happened before other than at His birth. But then it was the angels who were singing, and now for the first time the heavens opened and the voice of the Father was heard: "This is My beloved Son in whom I am well pleased." I often put it very crudely, but I think you will get the point. It was almost as if the Father said, "Like Father, like Son; this is My Son. The cross is in My heart, and now He has committed Himself to it at thirty years of age." Then the Holy Spirit fell upon Him. But just wait. Jesus was born of the Spirit. He was already indwelt of the Holy Spirit. Now something else happened. At thirty years of age, the age of Levitical and priestly service, the Holy Spirit fell on Him. He was born of the Spirit, indwelt of the Holy Spirit, He had the fruit of the Spirit, He was like His Father, and now the Holy Spirit fell on Him and anointed Him.

The Anointing of the Spirit

I have heard a whole number of messages during my life about the Holy Spirit being like a dove, and these messages are always about how sweet and gentle and meek a dove is, and how easily frightened a dove is. I am not being irreverent, but doves are very stupid birds. They are very sweet, very gentle, but they are incredibly stupid. They will lay an egg on a rafter and, of course, it falls off. They are not very clever. So why did the Holy Spirit come, as it says in one of the other gospels, in bodily form as a dove? It was not just meekness; Jesus was already meek. It was not just gentleness; He was gentle. What was it? The dove was the most normal form of sacrifice. If you were middle class, you brought a lamb or a goat. If you were wealthier, you brought a bullock, but the vast number of the poor brought two turtledoves. As soon as John saw the Holy Spirit falling on the Lord Jesus as a dove, he understood it: "Behold the Lamb of God who bears away the sin of the world." Here is God's sacrifice; it is the cross.

The Holy Spirit came upon the Lord Jesus to enable Him to die daily for three years, and then finally to be the ultimate, complete, absolute sacrifice for sin. It was by the eternal Spirit that Jesus offered Himself up to God without spot or blemish. The Holy Spirit came upon the Lord Jesus that He might enter the service that He was destined for, that He might fulfil the purpose in His coming. This is always the purpose of the Holy Spirit coming upon a child of God. It is not for our satisfaction. It is not for our fulness. It is not for some kind of personal aggrandizement. It is not for building some empire of our own. The Holy Spirit comes upon a child of God to enable that one to die daily.

It was as if the Holy Spirit came upon the Lord Jesus that He could bear, spiritually, the crossbeam of the cross for three years. Do you understand? You always see these pictures of a great cross, but there was no such thing. The stake was always in place. Sometimes it was a tree; sometimes it was just a great stake. But those sentenced to be crucified bore the crossbeam on their shoulders, and around their neck was hung a card with the sentence of death written on it. This is what the apostle Paul meant when he said, "We have the sentence of death within ourselves that we should not trust in ourselves but in God who raises the dead" (II Corinthians 1:9). We have the sentence of death and we are on our way to the place of execution. When the Holy Spirit came upon the Lord Jesus, it was to enable Him to bear the crossbeam for three years in all His actions, in all His responses, in everything He did.

Beloved brothers and sisters, what do we learn from this? I say this reverently. First, the Messiah needed the Holy Spirit to die daily. The Messiah needed the Holy Spirit in order for Him to finally go through to the cross. He needed the Holy Spirit in order to offer Himself up without spot or blemish, to become the source of eternal salvation for all of us who put our trust in Him.

Second, we need not only the indwelling of the Holy Spirit, we need the anointing of the Holy Spirit. The indwelling of the Holy Spirit brings fruit; the anointing of the Holy Spirit brings power—the ability to overcome, the ability to fulfil God's purpose in your life, the ability to become a watershed of rivers of living water. You cannot divide the Holy Spirit and say, "I will have the indwelling of the Holy Spirit, but I will not have the anointing of the Holy Spirit." The anointing of the Holy Spirit is absolutely essential. Every single thing that was of God in the temple was anointed. Everything! God would not use anything that was not anointed. God will not use an unanointed Christian because then it is their flesh that is doing the work; it is their unbroken energy, their own talents and gifts. Every single thing in the tabernacle was anointed—the altar of burnt offering, the laver, the lampstand, the shewbread table, incense, the ark of the covenant, the tent of meeting, the priests, the Levites, the prophets, the king—everyone was anointed. There was no such thing as anything unanointed.

There may be some who go overboard on this matter and do the weirdest and strangest things. There may be many things that are taught which are not biblical, but the fact remains that every child of God needs to be indwelt by the Holy Spirit and anointed by the Holy Spirit.

There is another thing. We cannot carry the cross without the Holy Spirit. Try it. Please, try it, and see if you can carry the cross without the Holy Spirit. What you will have is religion—sad, miserable, inward turned, defeated religion. Andrew Murray said,

"The Spirit leads to the cross and the cross leads to the Spirit." I know of no one who is crucified and living a crucified life who is not anointed. It is just religion, and there is an awful lot of religion in many of us. We know all the teaching about the cross, but we are still filled with jealousy, gossip, backbiting, rivalry, factions, worldliness, and a thousand and one other things. We can speak about the cross, sing about the cross, but without the Holy Spirit it never becomes a reality. Why? It is because the deepest instinct in the human being is self-preservation. We need the incredible power of the Holy Spirit to overcome that instinct of self-preservation, to help us to fall into the ground and die. We can never fulfil our ministry, we can never fulfil God's purpose without the anointing of the Holy Spirit.

I know very well what I tried to do. I tried to minister to people; I tried to teach them; I tried to save them, to convert them. What a mess I got myself into! It was all religion. Of course, I thought it was what a Christian ought to do. I came from a non-Christian background. So I thought this was what a Christian ought to do, but it did not work. I found it to be the heaviest thing in the whole world to be a Christian. It was only when I was with everybody else singing wonderful hymns that I felt a bit better. But as soon as I was on my own that awful heaviness came back. So then I would redouble my efforts to be a good Christian, and I made the situation far worse. When the Lord opened the heaven for me and suddenly I saw that the Holy Spirit was in me and on me, I saw Pentecost as a historic fact, and once for all I could enter into it. It is mine! I had no idea it was mine. In that moment I gave the keys to the Holy Spirit, and then suddenly realized I was crucified with Christ. I had never heard of such a thing.

It was the greatest relief I have ever experienced as a Christian. I did not have to try anymore; I just sank back and became myself. Isn't that unbelievable to say that as a Christian I became myself? That is how it began.

If you have any argument with me, let me say this. If the Lord Jesus, who was born of the Holy Spirit and indwelt by the Holy Spirit needed the anointing of the Holy Spirit to fulfil His ministry, so do you and so do I. I think that settles the argument.

The Transfiguration of the Christ

The second thing is the transfiguration of the Lord Jesus. I think it is amazing what happened in that transfiguration. We often think of the transfiguration as a kind of spotlight that shone on the Lord Jesus, like a searchlight. It suddenly found Him and He was sort of lit up by a searchlight, by a spotlight, as if the light was focused on Him and made Him very bright. But that is not what happened in the transfiguration. It was a change that took place. Something was switched on inside. It was the glory of God. Suddenly the glory of God did not just shine on Him; it shone out of Him, and He was transfigured. His face shone like the sun. His clothes radiated light. (People often ask me: "Are we going to wear anything in the glory?" I do not often get the Chinese asking me that question. I get Germans and Scandinavians asking me that. The Chinese always ask me: "Are we going to eat?") This glory shone out of the Lord Jesus. It was as if somehow or other something happened to His being.

What is transfiguration? It is the glory of God from within, transforming the human being, changing them, and yet they are still the same. Something happens. The Lord Jesus was not transfigured as God the Son; He was transfigured as the Son of Man.

In 1 Corinthians 15:45–47 it speaks of Him as the last Adam:

So also it is written, The first man Adam became a living soul. The last Adam became a life-giving spirit. Howbeit that is not first which is spiritual, but that which is natural; then that which is spiritual. The first man is of the earth, earthy; the second man is of heaven.

The Lord Jesus was not the second Adam; He was the last Adam. He finished it all. When He went to the cross, He not only died to save us but He died as us. He took Adam to the cross. The Lord Jesus is the last Adam, but He is the second Man. Adam was the first man; Jesus is the second Man. And the Lord Jesus as Man succeeded where the first man fell. It says in Roman 3:23:

"For all have sinned and fallen short of the glory of God."

If Adam had taken of the tree of life instead of the tree of the knowledge of good and evil, there would have been a whole training period, a probation period. He would have learned obedience by the things which he suffered. If he had come through, Adam and Eve would have been transfigured in glory, and the whole story of this world and of mankind would have been different. But he fell short of the glory of God and disobeyed Him. He ate from the tree that was forbidden.

People often argue about what the tree was. Was it an apple tree? Was it an orange tree? Was it an apricot? Some think it was a mango. It would not have mattered if it had been a rose bush. The point is that the Lord said, "Don't eat of that tree." It was not the taste; it was not the fruit; it was the disobedience. That was the key to falling short of the glory of God.

The Lord Jesus came as the second Man, and He was tempted in all points like as we are yet was without sin. He succeeded where the first man failed, and at that point the Lord Jesus could have stepped into heaven. He could have ascended to the throne of God, and there would have been one Man in the glory, one Man who succeeded where all the rest failed. This is where we see the cross in the Lord Jesus before He even came to Calvary. He turned away and set His face toward Jerusalem.

It is very interesting that almost immediately a multitude came to Him, and a father, almost out of His mind, said, "Oh, I brought my son to your disciples and they could not do anything. He is filled with something, and he foams at the mouth. He rolls on the floor and damages himself. Can You do anything? While Jesus turned to the boy, the boy had at that point an exceedingly powerful convulsion" (see Matthew 17:14–18). This is a picture of the world we live in—demonized. At one moment so intelligent, so sophisticated, so clever, so creative, so beautiful, and the next moment wallowing on the ground, foaming at the mouth, caught by another power, something Satanic, something destructive, something out of which that poor boy could not escape, and over which the disciples were paralysed. What a picture of the church! What a picture of the world! It would have been easier for the

Lord Jesus to have stepped into the throne of God, but instead, He turned and deliberately came down and threw the demon out of the little boy. In one sense that is what God has done for every one of us. He has thrown out the devil. He has delivered us from the power and authority of darkness and transferred us into the kingdom of His dear Son. How did He do it? It was not by the transfiguration, although that was important, but by the cross. There is no other way.

Gethsemane—Victory Won by the Christ

Lastly, Gethsemane. It is my conviction that the Lord Jesus won the battle of Calvary, not on Calvary but in Gethsemane. Once He won the battle in Gethsemane He was calm, and He could go forward. He could stand before Pontius Pilate, before the religious leaders, before King Herod and before that crowd of brutal Roman soldiers. He went through it all. When they nailed His hands to the cross, He said, "Forgive them, Father, they do not know what they are doing." What a prayer! The Father answered it; some of those soldiers got saved. It is an amazing, amazing way in which the Lord Jesus faced the cross once He won the battle in Gethsemane.

What happened in Gethsemane? *Gethsemane* means simply in Hebrew "oil press." What happened in that garden? Was Jesus afraid of the pain? Look at Him. He did not just stand and pray which is the normal Jewish way to pray. He did not just kneel which is another way to pray. He fell prostrate on His face, and said, "Father, if this cup can pass from Me, let it; nevertheless, not as I will but as Thou wilt." What was it that seized the Lord Jesus? Why was He so distressed? After all, He knew from eternity that it was the cross that would be the fulfilment. Thus, He was born to die. Why did He suddenly have those second thoughts?

So great was the trauma through which Jesus went that He said, "My soul is exceeding sorrowful to the point of death." That was not just Jewish exaggeration. Luke tells us that He sweat drops like blood, and medical authorities tell us that there is a form of trauma in which blood actually comes out in perspiration and is nearly always just before death.

There were two things that happened in the garden. The first was this: Satan brought before Jesus all the horrors of one who was sinless being made sin. Satan is a past master at this. He brought before the Lord Jesus vision after vision after vision—all the sin in the world being piled upon one person. That sin of Hitler, Stalin, Mao Tse-Tung, Saddam Hussein, and a thousand others. The whole of history from its beginning to its end, all that sin with all its evil gathered upon the Lord Jesus. For the Lord Jesus it was the unknown. Never before had He been divorced from His Father. Not for a moment in all His being had He ever been separated. Satan played on Him: "Wait until I get You and see what I will do."

Hebrews 5 tells us that He was heard; His prayer was heard. I believe that for the Lord Jesus it was not the torture, nor the ridicule, nor the nails, nor the physical ill treatment; it was the divorce from the Father when He was made sin for us. Let it sink in—made sin for us, made our sin. That is the first thing. For a moment the Lord Jesus said, "Father, is there not another way?" I do not believe for a moment that Jesus believed that. He knew there was no other way. That is why He almost immediately said, "Not as I will but as Thou will." He knew there was no other way.

The second thing was that Satan tried to kill Him in the garden. I believe it. I believe that Satan tried to bring Jesus into such a trauma that He could have died, and He would never have gone to Calvary. The Father sent an angel and told him: "Get down there immediately. Strengthen Him and don't let this trauma kill Him. Don't let My enemy win." Almost immediately Jesus got up and said, "You can sleep; I have won!"

This is the cross and the Messiah. When next you break bread and drink the wine, remember that this is what it cost your Lord to save you. This is what He had to suffer that you and I might be apathetic, lukewarm, affluent, undevoted, self-pleasing, selfish.

Dear family of God, not in all eternity will we ever know what it really cost the Lord Jesus to win, not even when we have been there a million, million, million years. We are created beings with finite minds. Not even in eternity will we ever really know what it cost the Lord Jesus. But this we know: in that garden He won the battle, and He went forward with absolute calmness. He never lost that calmness until the darkness came across the whole earth and He cried out, "My God, My God, why has Thou forsaken Me?" The unknown had become His experience. The moment that He had feared so much in the garden, in that moment it became His experience.

Don't despise your salvation! Don't treat the love of God for you lightly as if you deserve it! What arrogance! Your Lord loved you so much and He went through all of this for you. He did not need to, for He had already been glorified. He could have reached the throne as a Man alone, but He wanted to bring many sons to glory.

May our hearts be touched. We are Laodiceans, and we do not understand our real condition in the sight of God. Many of us do not hear the voice of the Lord. We have so much knowledge up here, but it actually makes us deaf to His voice. May the Lord touch our hearts, humble us, bring us to repentance, and bring us back into first love.

Shall we pray:

What shall we say, Lord? Forgive us. We often have so little idea in the busy lives we live, the routine we have. We never stop to think: What did it cost You? We even come to Your table and break bread and drink the cup, and it is routine and yet You said, Lord, "Do this in an affectionate bringing to mind of what I did." Lord, touch our hearts. We ask it in the name of the Lord Jesus. Amen.

3.
Yes, Even the Death of the Cross

Philippians 2:1–13
If there is therefore any exhortation in Christ, if any consolation of love, if any fellowship of the Spirit, if any tender mercies and compassions, make full my joy, that ye be of the same mind, having the same love, being of one accord, of one mind; doing nothing through faction or through vainglory, but in lowliness of mind each counting other better than himself; not looking each of you to his own things, but each of you also to the things of others. Have this mind in you, which was also in Christ Jesus: who, existing in the form of God, counted not the being on an equality with God a thing to be grasped, but emptied himself, taking the form of a bondslave, being made in the likeness of men; and being found in fashion as a man, he humbled himself, becoming obedient even unto death, yea, the death of the cross. Wherefore also God highly exalted him and gave unto him the name which is above every name; that at the name of Jesus

every knee should bow, of things in heaven and things on earth and things under the earth, and that every tongue should confess that Jesus Christ is Lord, to the glory of God the Father.

So then, my beloved, even as ye have always obeyed, not as in my presence only, but now much more in my absence, work out your own salvation with fear and trembling; for it is God who worketh in you both to will and to work, for his good pleasure.

Revelation 5:5–10

And one of the elders saith unto me, Weep not; behold, the Lion that is of the tribe of Judah, the Root of David, hath overcome to open the book and the seven seals thereof. And I saw in the midst of the throne and of the four living creatures, and in the midst of the elders, a Lamb standing, as though it had been slain, having seven horns, and seven eyes, which are the seven Spirits of God, sent forth into all the earth. And he came, and he taketh it out of the right hand of him that sat on the throne. And when he had taken the book, the four living creatures and the four and twenty elders fell down before the Lamb, having each one a harp, and golden bowls full of incense, which are the prayers of the saints. And they sing a new song, saying, Worthy art thou to take the book, and to open the seals thereof: for thou wast slain, and didst purchase unto God with thy blood men of every tribe, and tongue, and people, and nation, and madest them to be unto our God a kingdom and priest; and they reign upon the earth.

Shall we pray:

Beloved Lord, we are once again so thankful to You for the way that You have led us through these days. Now we come to this time, and we know that You have made full provision for it. We thank You for Your faithfulness, for Your love, and for Your mercy. Beloved Lord, we need You. We need You for the speaking of Your Word, for the translating of Your Word, and for the hearing of Your Word. Don't let this time pass without touching our hearts. Somehow reach us in the deepest part of our being. Let Your Holy Spirit open the eyes of our heart and bring us to a new place of response to You. To that end we stand by faith into that anointing grace and power You have made available to us. Let it be upon us all in full power, and we shall be careful to give You all the praise and all the glory. We ask it in the name of our Lord Jesus the Messiah. Amen.

My responsibility has been the cross and the Christ, and I want to take one or two phrases from the Word of God for this time. I want to speak about the phrase, "Yes, even the death of the cross." Then I want to speak about the phrase, "Wherefore also God has highly exalted Him." Then finally, "Work out your own salvation with fear and trembling, for it is God who worketh in you to will and to work for His good pleasure."

The Death of the Cross

There was no other way that the Lord Jesus could fulfill God's eternal purpose, and in six hours, only six hours, He accomplished this work. At nine o'clock in the morning He was nailed to the cross; at three in the afternoon He died. It was the six most significant, most strategic, and most vital hours of time. Not only of time, it is the focal point of eternity. So amazing is the work of our Lord Jesus! For this, He came into the world. For this, at some point He said to the Father, "Here am I, send Me." For this reason He was born in Bethlehem, born to die. For this reason He was baptised in the River Jordan by John. For this reason He turned from His transfiguration in glory to make His way to Jerusalem to die. For this cause in the garden, He said, "Not My will but Thine be done." *Six hours.* I think it is an enormous mistake to dwell upon the physical sufferings of the Lord Jesus. If it was the physical sufferings of the Lord Jesus alone that worked our salvation, many martyrs have died and suffered for a far longer time. I remember the case of a pastor who was crucified in China, and it took three days for him to die.

What happened in those six hours? It is amazing to me how reticent the gospel witnesses are. It is almost as if they do not want to dwell for too long upon the physical suffering of the Lord Jesus. They just describe the facts that He was nailed to the cross, He thirsted, He cried out and finally said, "Into Your hands I commit My Spirit." It is almost as if they felt that somehow it was not what was seen that worked our salvation but what was not seen. It was there in the invisible that Jesus was made sin for us. In all the years of eternity we will never know how much it cost the Lord Jesus. We stand on the shore of an ocean of unutterable, incomprehensible agony. Think of some of the Scriptures.

> *Behold, the Lamb of God, who beareth away*
> *the sin of the world. (John 1:29)*

*All we like sheep have gone astray; we have turned
every one to his own way; and the Lord hath laid
on him the iniquity of us all. (Isaiah 53:6)*

The Hebrew is graphic: "And the Lord caused all the iniquity to encounter Him." It is better understood this way, "All the iniquity gathered upon Him." From the sin of Adam, from the sin of Cain, all the way through history, all sin was gathered upon the Person of the Lord Jesus in those few hours.

The Little Lamb and the Snake

There is something so beautiful about a lamb. It is a symbol of new life, a symbol of innocence, a symbol of purity, a symbol of a new beginning. There is something so beautiful about a little lamb, and something so dark, so horrific about iniquity. When that iniquity was gathered upon that little Lamb, then He became the serpent lifted up. There is nothing more different from a little lamb than a snake. I know some people keep snakes as pets, but I have a horror of them, especially when I see people with them all around their necks. There is something so devious and sinister about the snake.

In John 3:14 it says,

*Even as Moses lifted up the serpent in the wilderness,
even so must the Son of Man be lifted up, that whosoever
believeth on him should have everlasting life.*

There is something so different about a lamb and a serpent, but the Lord Jesus took into Himself the very poison of Satan.

That poison which has infected the whole of mankind He took into Himself. We will never know how much that sin affected the Lord Jesus. All we know is that He bore it away. He took it into Himself and bore it away, just as the scapegoat went out into the wilderness. He removed our sin as far as the East is from the West and blotted it out as a thick cloud; He cancelled it. Just as the apostle Paul said, "He who knew no sin was made sin for us that we sinners might become the righteousness of God in Him" (II Corinthians 5:21).

What happened in those six hours? There is another little cameo in Isaiah 53:10: "It pleased the Lord to bruise Him." The Hebrew means, "It pleased the Lord to crush Him." The Hebrew means "to break into pieces, to trample underfoot." It pleased the Lord to crush Him. In those hours He took into Himself the sin of the world from the beginning to the end. The Lamb became the uplifted serpent, and God crushed Him. Is it any wonder that He cried out: "My God, My God, why hast Thou forsaken Me?" It was that which in the garden had caused Him such distress.

We see perhaps the mystery of this most clearly in the darkness that came over the earth. At noon darkness came over the whole area. People who do not understand these things say it was an eclipse, but anyone who knows anything about eclipses knows that no eclipse can ever last three hours. Something happened to the essential energy of the universe, as if a sword went through the heart of God Himself. When Jesus was made sin and was crushed—the very essence of the word "all things exist in Him"— it caused the whole universe to shudder. Light became darkness. Six hours—the death of the cross.

A Full Salvation for Whosoever

In Hebrews 2:9 it is written,

> *But we behold him who hath been made a little lower than the angels, even Jesus, because of the suffering of death crowned with glory and honour, that by the grace of God he should taste of death for everyone.*

If the Lord Jesus had only died in my place alone, it would have been tremendous for me, but when He died, He tasted death for everyone—every man and woman who has ever lived or who will ever live. We shall never understand what happened, nor would it be right for us to speculate. But this we know, He finished the work that the Father gave Him. In those six hours He accomplished eternal salvation—so complete that nothing can be added to it and nothing taken away. It is so full a salvation that the most depraved sinner can be saved, the most hopeless human being can be turned into a child of God, those who have no right to inherit anything of God might inherit everything. It is not by all our tears or all our knowledge of the Bible or all our church going or all our church ceremonies that we can ever achieve salvation. We are not saved because our parents were Christians, or our grandparents were Christians, or we have relatives and friends who are Christians. We are saved only by the finished work of the Lord Jesus on Calvary. That has to become the living, personal, direct experience of every human being if he or she is to be saved. He won for us in six hours a place in God's eternal purpose.

God's eternal purpose is not salvation. God's salvation is the means by which He puts us back into His eternal purpose.

When the Lord Jesus accomplished our eternal salvation in those six hours, He provided for us all the grace and power we need to come to the heart of His eternal purpose. It is so sad that so few Christians understand the death of the cross. How much He loved us!

God Highly Exalted Him

We come to the second phrase in Philippians 2:9–11:

> *Wherefore also God highly exalted him, and gave unto him the name which is above every name; that at the name of Jesus every knee should bow, of things in heaven and things on earth and things under the earth, and that every tongue should confess that Jesus Christ is Lord, to the glory of God the Father.*

What a wonderful power is in this one word "wherefore"! "Wherefore God highly exalted him." Why did God exalt Him so highly? Because He did not think being on an equality with God a thing to be grasped or fought for, but He humbled Himself and became a bondslave and being found in the form of a man He became obedient even unto death, the death of the cross.

Now I was always taught that if the Word of God said something more than once you should take note of it. Listen to this:

A Bondslave

> *Humble yourselves in the sight of the Lord, and he shall exalt you. (James 4:10)*

But he that is greatest among you shall be your bondslave. And whosoever shall exalt himself shall be humbled; and whosoever shall humble himself shall be exalted.(Matthew 23:11–12)

For every one that exalteth himself shall be humbled; and he that humbleth himself shall be exalted. (Luke 14:11)

I say unto you, This man went down to his house justified rather than the other: for every one that exalteth himself shall be humbled; but he that humbleth himself shall be exalted. (Luke 18:14:)

When the Lord Jesus humbled Himself, we have a picture, an amazing illustration of this principle: whenever a person humbles himself or herself, the Lord will exalt them. The Lord Jesus is the supreme example. He does not ask you to do anything that He has not done Himself. He that will be the greatest among you, let him be a bondslave—no rights, completely given. Wouldn't it transform our fellowships, our assemblies, if everyone who wants to be great became a bondslave? Wouldn't it be tremendous if we gave up our rights in order to care for one another, to serve one another, to commit ourselves to the Lord in one another? If we were to humble ourselves, what exalting there would be by the Lord!

The Altar

It is very interesting that you have two pictures in the Bible of a great river. In the prophecy of Ezekiel in chapter 47, he saw the temple of the Lord, and out from the altar on the right side came a stream of water. As it flowed it went from the ankles to the knees, to the thighs, and then water to swim in. Everywhere that the river came in Ezekiel's vision it brought life. It even healed the Dead Sea. There is nothing that lives in the Dead Sea—not a plant, not a fish, not a crab, not a crayfish, nothing. Nothing! It is sterile; but when this river which comes out of the altar flows into the Dead Sea, a miracle takes place. There will be a great multitude of fish that come into these waters, and fishermen will stand by it and spread their nets, and on either side of the river are trees bearing fruit. It all comes from the altar.

The Throne

There is another picture at the very end of the Bible. It is in the last chapter of Revelation, and it is the city of God. God and the Lamb are the temple and out of the throne flows a river. Wherever this river goes it brings healing. Its fruit and its leaves are for the healing of the nations. The altar has become the throne. That is always God's way—first the altar and then the throne. The Lord Jesus humbled Himself, becoming a bondslave, and being found in the fashion of a man, He was obedient even unto death, yes the death of the cross. Wherefore also God has highly exalted Him, enthroned Him at His right hand, until every knee shall bow to Him and every tongue confess Him as Lord. It is a wonderful picture. The altar has become the throne.

What an amazing picture we have in Revelation 5 of a little Lamb in the midst of the throne! The Greek is "as if freshly slain." Here is the throne of God; here is the throne of the universe, and in the midst of the throne is a little Lamb, as if freshly slain.

It is the power of those six hours, the power of that finished work reaching back to the foundation of the world, reaching forward to the ages of ages because of a little Lamb, the Lion of the tribe of Judah. It is a little Lamb as if freshly slain that is the foundation for all of God's dealings with mankind from Adam to the last person who will ever be born.

Listen to the four and twenty elders and the four living ones: "Worthy art thou, for with thy blood You have purchased from every tongue and ethnic group and race a people for Yourself." Worthy! No one else is as worthy to be the King as Jesus. No other king has ever given his life for the salvation of his people. I often say to my own people, the Jewish people: "He is our King. He is King of the Jews and King of Israel." Israel thinks she is a republic, but actually she is a kingdom. She is the only nation in the world who has a King who died to save, who was buried and on the third day rose. Then He ascended to the right hand of God as Saviour of the world, as Head of the church, as King of the Jews, King of Israel, King of kings and Lord of lords. No other people have such a history. We have a King who died, who rose again, who is at the right hand of God and is going to return to Jerusalem. Who else is worthy to be ruler of the kings of the earth, worthy to be King of kings and Lord of lords? There is no one else, only Jesus.

Work out Your Own Salvation with Fear and Trembling

The way to the fulfilment of God's eternal purpose is the cross and the work that Jesus did in those six hours. Do you not find it amazing that after this tremendous revelation of the Lord Jesus, Paul says, "So then work out your own salvation with fear and trembling"? You cannot work out your own salvation without the cross. It is impossible! There is a divine veto on any kind of working out of your salvation if it is without the cross. You can only be saved through His work on the cross, but until your self-life is laid down, you cannot see that salvation worked out in your life. "For it is God that worketh in you both to will and to work of His good pleasure." Where there is an uncrucified self-life there is no God working in you both to will and to work. "Oh," you say, "this is too severe. We want something more gentle, more loving than this."

Take Up the Cross

The Lord Jesus says in Mark 8:34–35:

And he called unto him the multitude with his disciples, and said unto them, If any man would come after me, let him deny himself, and take up his cross, and follow me. For whosoever would save his life shall lose it; and whosoever shall lose his life for my sake and the gospel's shall save it.

You cannot follow the Lord and love your self-life. You cannot follow the Lord without taking up your cross. It is impossible! You cannot live the Christian life and love your self-life. If you seek to preserve it, you paralyse the work of the Holy Spirit, you grieve the Holy Spirit, you quench the Holy Spirit, and you put the fire out. That is what happens when our fellowships are filled with people thinking about themselves. *I, I, I.* Only when *I* is crossed out, then you have the body of the Lord Jesus, then you have the building up of the house of God, then you have an expression of the Lord Jesus that turns the world upside down.

Every assembly should be seeing people saved and added to the church. What is it? *I* is the problem. Jesus preached this gospel to the whole multitude, not just to His disciples: "If any man come after me, let him give up all right to himself, take up the crossbeam, and follow Me. Whosoever would save his life, his self-life, his soul-life is the word in Greek, shall lose it" (see Luke 9:23–24). How many Christians are losing their soul, who are fighting for their self-life? You are losing it by seeking to safe-guard it. You are losing it and with it, the whole expression of the body of Christ. You cannot follow the Lord Jesus without the cross. You cannot come into the fulness of life, abundant life without the cross. If you do not humble yourself, in the end God will humble you. It is one of the most extraordinary things that the Lord always says, "Humble yourself." It is just like the Lord Jesus. He made the decision: "I will do the will of My Father."

I am sorry that it sounds so hard, so severe, but I do not apologize for it. It is the gospel as it ought to be preached. We hear this gospel: "Make a decision for the Lord Jesus" as if it is a presidential election. "You vote for Him, you make Him your president, and He will do you good. He will help you, clean up the messes, follow you, support you, and do everything for you. He will be your insurance." It is this kind of gospel. Then, when we make a decision, He is there for us. My Jesus is there for me. I can do my own thing, and when I am in a mess, I go back to Him and He cleans it up. Your will always will get you into a mess.

The Self-Life is Ground for Satanic Working

What a thing the Lord Jesus said to Peter. When the Lord Jesus spoke about His cross, Peter said, "God have mercy on You; be it far from You." And Jesus, turning around, looked into his eyes and said, "Get behind Me, Satan" (see Matthew 16:22–23). If I looked into your eyes and said, "Get behind Me, Satan," you would be very upset. You would say, "That is not the way to say things. We need loving brothers, not someone who looks into our eyes and says, 'Get behind Me, Satan.'" If only Jesus had said, "Simon, Satan is troubling your mind." That would have been so real, so good. If He had said, "You are not seeing it quite right, Peter." But He looked into his eyes and said to this chief apostle, "Get behind Me, Satan. You do not mind the things of God but the things of man." His self-life was the ground for satanic working. *So is yours.* That self-life of yours that you mollycoddle, that you love, that you hug, that you feed, that you seek to fulfil, will destroy you. It has the poison of Satan within it, and it will destroy you. It will destroy your family, your fellowship, and your service for the Lord. That is why the Lord Jesus said, "If any man come after Me, let him give up all right to himself, take up his crossbeam and follow Me. He that loses his self-life for My sake and the gospel's will find it."

Listen to what the Lord Jesus said to the church at Laodicea: "If any man hear My voice and open the door, I will come in and sup with him and he with Me." It is a beautiful picture—a meal, communion, fellowship. "If any man hear My voice and open the door, I will come into him and will sup with him and he with Me. He that overcomes shall sit down with Me in My throne, as I also overcame and sat down with My Father in His throne" (see Revelation 3:20–21). The way to the throne is to hear what Jesus is saying. You will never come to the throne if you are not prepared to be a bondslave.

Present Your Bodies

When the apostle Paul, by the Spirit of God, wrote the greatest exposition of the gospel that we have in the sixty-six books of the Bible, this is how he ended Romans: "I beseech you therefore, brethren, that you go out and evangelise." No. That would be quite right, but he did not say that. "I beseech you therefore, brethren, by the mercies of God that you always be present at the prayer meeting." Very important, but he did not say that. "I beseech you therefore, brethren, that you get to know your Bible." Absolutely essential, but he did not say that. This is what he said. "I beseech you therefore, brethren, by the mercies of God, to present your bodies a living sacrifice, holy, acceptable to God, which is your spiritually intelligent service and worship."

When you receive the gospel, how should it end? You present your body a living sacrifice by the mercies of God expressed toward you. If only we could hear! If you have an argument with another believer, humble yourself, and go and ask for forgiveness. If you have misrepresented someone, ask the Lord to forgive you. Humble yourself. Where there is fighting, let it stop. Where there is murmuring, let it cease. "Have this mind in you, which was also in the Messiah Jesus; who being on an equality with God did not think it a thing to be grasped, but humbled Himself taking the form of a bondslave, and being found in fashion as a man, He became obedient even to death, yes the death of the cross. Wherefore also God highly exalted Him" (see Philippians 2:5–9).

This is the way to the fulfilment of God's eternal purpose in your life. This is the way to the fulfilment of God's eternal purpose in us as believers, building us up as the body of Christ, living stones built together. This is the way that you and I can serve the Lord.

Shall we pray:

Beloved Lord, we just bow before You. We know none of us are worthy, and in this matter of our self-life we have to say that nearly all of us are failing. Challenge us, confront us by Your Holy Spirit. We cannot follow You unless we give up all right to ourselves. Help us, Lord, to will Your will, and we know You will take care of the execution. Help us, Lord. We ask it in the name of our Lord Jesus. Amen.

4.
Love Not the World

Galatians 6:14

But far be it from me to glory, save in the cross of our Lord Jesus Christ, through which the world hath been crucified unto me, and I unto the world.

Ephesians 2:1–5

And you did he make alive, when ye were dead through your trespasses and sins, wherein ye once walked according to the course of this world, according to the prince of the powers of the air, of the spirit that now worketh in the sons of disobedience; among whom we also all once lived in the lusts of our flesh, doing the desires of the flesh and of the mind, and were by nature children of wrath, even as the rest:—but God, being rich in mercy, for his great love wherewith he loved us, even when we were dead through our trespasses, made us alive together with Christ (by grace have ye been saved).

1 John 2:15–17

Love not the world, neither the things that are in the world. If any man love the world, the love of the Father is not in him. For all that is in the world, the lust of the flesh and the lust of the eyes, and the vainglory of life, is not of the Father, but is of the world. And the world passeth away, and the lust thereof: but he that doeth the will of God abideth forever.

Colossians 1:19–23

For it was the good pleasure of the Father that in him [Christ] should all the fullness dwell; and through him to reconcile all things unto himself, having made peace through the blood of his cross; through him, I say, whether things upon the earth, or things in the heaven. And you, being in time pass alienated and enemies in your mind in your evil works, yet now hath he reconciled in the body of his flesh through death, to present you holy and without blemish and unreprovable before him: if so be that ye continue in the faith, grounded and steadfast, and not moved away from the hope of the gospel which ye heard, which was preached in all creation under heaven: whereof I Paul was made a minister

Can we just have a further word of prayer:

Beloved Lord, we are glad that we are found here in Your presence, and we want very simply, as we come to the ministry of Your Word, to confess that without You we can do nothing. Beloved Lord, we need that anointing which You alone can give, and we thank You that You have not left us without provision for such a time as this. Through the finished work of our Lord Jesus, You have at great cost provided us with an anointing and made it a glorious reality in the Person of the Holy Spirit. Therefore, beloved Lord, by faith we stand into that anointing grace and power for both the speaking of Your Word, the translating of it, and the hearing of it. Pierce our hearts, Lord. Somehow meet us and challenge us. Don't let us be the same. Lord, we are living in incredibly dangerous days. Everything is happening so fast and rapidly deteriorating. We need You, Lord. Speak to our hearts we pray, and we ask it in the name of our Lord Jesus, the Messiah. Amen.

The theme for these gatherings continues from last year: "The Way to the Eternal Purpose of God—the Cross." There is *no* alternative to the cross. The only way a human being can be saved is through the work of our Lord Jesus on the cross. The only way this world can be redeemed, that is the physical world, is through the cross of our Lord Jesus. There is no other way for any child of God to be changed into the likeness of the Lord Jesus. It is simplicity itself and because it is so simple, we all overlook it. We get into such a theological complexity, when Christ crucified is the only way that God has ordained.

What Is the World?

I will be sharing in these few days on the cross and the world. I find this a very difficult subject because of the complexity of the way the word *world* is used in English. For instance, that verse in Galatians 6: "But far be it from me to glory, save in the cross of our Lord Jesus the Messiah, through which the world has been crucified unto me, and I unto the world."

The Greek word used here is *cosmos*. There are two words that are translated into English by the same word *world*. One is *cosmos*. This is the whole material universe. Everything within it, all the beauty that is in it, all the human beings that inhabit it make up the total material universe.

The other word is *eon*. In English we speak of the "eons of time." This word is sometimes translated age, ages, or periods. It has the feeling of something continuous. In the Ephesian letter of the apostle Paul, chapter 2:2, we have both words used. This is how he writes it: "Wherein ye once walked according to the course of this world." The word translated *course* in English is *age, eon* "... according to the *age* of this world." Quite rightly they have translated it in the 1901 American Standard Version, "according to the *course* of this world, the *duration* of this world." Something has happened, and both these words have acquired, in general, an unfavourable meaning in the Bible.

Consider for instance, Galatians 1:4: "Who gave Himself for our sins, that He might deliver us out of this present evil world [age], according to the will of our God and Father."

Then, as we've already said, in Ephesians 2:2–3: "Wherein ye once walked according to the course of this world [cosmos]." Then he goes on to describe this world: "According to the prince of the powers of the air, of the spirit that now worketh in the sons of disobedience; among whom we also all once lived in the lusts of our flesh, doing the desires of the flesh and of the mind, and were by nature children of wrath."

The same idea is in the first letter of the apostle John, chapter 2:15: "Love not the world neither the things that are in the world. If any man love the world, the love of the Father is not in him."

The word here is *cosmos*. "Love not the world and the things that are within the world." What does John mean? Think of what God Himself said in John 3:16a, "For God so loved the world [cosmos]." Something has happened to this world. That is what I mean when I said these two Greek words, on the whole, have acquired a very unfavourable, almost dark meaning in the Word of God. Of course, John was always black and white; there were never any shades between the two. But he goes on to explain himself: "For all that is in the world, the lust of the flesh and the lust of the eyes and the vainglory of life, is not of the Father, but is of the world. And the world passeth away" (1 John 2:16–17a).

Then again, look at the book of James who was another very stark person. This is how he puts it in James 4:4, speaking to Christians: "Ye adulteresses, know ye not that the friendship of the world is enmity with God? Whosoever therefore would be a friend of the world maketh himself an enemy of God."

These are tough words, exceedingly severe. "You adulteresses, you have broken your marriage covenant with God. You have given yourself to another spirit, a worldly spirit, the spirit that is in this world." Then he uses the word *enmity*. I like better the New American Standard Bible translation *hostility*. It is the same idea, an enemy of God. Rather strong, isn't it?

What Happened to This World?

This is the word that the Lord said as it is recorded in Genesis 1:31: "And God saw everything that He had made, and, behold, it was very good." What has happened to this world that God created? Apparently, when the world was first created, it was pure; it was the work of God. What then has happened? Well, we have the fall of Satan and a third of the angels, and the fall of man. This fall, beginning with Satan and the angels, and moving into Adam and Eve, and the human race, substantially and essentially changed and altered this world. Something entered into the world that was altogether other than God. You remember that the apostle Paul said, "We wrestle not against flesh and blood, but against principalities, against powers, against the world-rulers of this darkness, against hosts of wicked spirits in the heavenly places" (see Ephesians 6:12).

When God created man, he was the apex of the natural creation. I think of it as a triangle. At the very bottom are all the creatures that Darwin called primeval, but still created by God. Then you have the fish, the reptiles, the bugs, and all the other things as you come upwards. Then the birds, the animals, and the mammals, the nearest in one sense to the human being. Then came man. That was a triangle. But the other triangle came down from heaven—Father, Son, and Holy Spirit. The idea was that the Spirit of God would dwell in that human being, and that the whole world would be governed and supervised by man.

This is not so crazy as it may seem. After all, how did Noah get all those animals into the ark? Have you ever thought about it? I have three dogs and three cats and it is hard enough to get them into the house. How did he get them in unless he was able to communicate? The fear of man was not in the animal creation until the flood.

When man fell, it was as if the hub of the wheel was torn out, as if the very heart of the practical energizing of the universe was destroyed. Man, instead of being a God-centred,

God-conscious, and God-dependent being became a self-centred, self-conscious, self-dependent being. And from that point, you have human history as we know it. It is man everywhere—*I, I, I;* my aggrandizement, my glory, and my fulfilment. It is everything to do with man. He builds empires for his glory which is humanism, the last great antichrist philosophy of this world—six, six, six—fallen man, fallen man, and everything in it, fallen man. God intends to sum up everything in Christ. In order to take man, Satan wants to sum up everything in man—fallen man, man in union with spirits and demons. This is no fairy tale. When man fell, the world acquired a new character. It was substantially and essentially altered. Nevertheless, I must tell you that this world is still very beautiful, but it has been essentially and substantially altered. It is indwelt by Satan.

Some of you may say that I am going a little too far. Really? Why do you think Satan is called the prince of this world? (See John 12:31.) Why do you think that all these things we read about happened to the world? Why did it change?

Genesis 3:17–19 says, "And unto Adam God said, Because thou hast harkened unto the voice of thy wife, and hath eaten of the tree, of which I commanded thee, saying, Thou shalt not eat of it: cursed is the ground for thy sake; in toil shalt thou eat of it all the days of thy life; thorns also and thistles shall it bring forth to thee; and thou shalt eat the herb of the field; in the sweat of thy face shalt thou eat bread, till thou return unto the ground; for out of it wast thou taken: for dust thou art, and unto dust shalt thou return."

Something happened when man fell—thorns and thistles. Sometimes, people come to me and say, "Were mosquitoes and flies a result of the fall? Were cockroaches, especially those huge ones, a result of the fall? Where did they all come from?" But if you were to say, "Take them out," the whole cycle of nature would be altered. However, something happened when man fell. In the first letter of John he says, "The whole world [cosmos] lieth in the evil one" (5:19b). We can still see such beauty in this world. When the beauty of this world first makes its impact upon us, we worship God. We also know that though man himself has fallen, we cannot forget that he was made in the image of God. There is still an imprint deep within the human being. Even when he is depraved, even when he is perverted, even when he is fallen, there is still the imprint. It is amazing!

This demonic change is most clearly seen in man. Romans 12:2 says, "And be not fashioned according to this world." This is not *cosmos*; this is *eon*. Be not fashioned, be not moulded, be not formed by this age. But we all are; we are in the mould. And even when we become Christians, so many find it impossible to get out of the mould. The apostle is speaking to believers, not the unsaved. He says, "Be not fashioned according to this world." Get out of the mould. Don't let this age form your outlook, your mindset.

"And be not fashioned according to this age, but be ye transformed by the renewing of your mind." That means another mindset. "Have this mind in you which was also in Christ Jesus." Follow it; for it is another mindset.

The Great Destroyer of the Church

Do you know what the biggest problem in the Christian life is? The mould of this world, the fashion of this world. It stunts the

Christian life, paralyses it, and spoils it. It finally corrupts it and in the end destroys it. Then you have become a monument, a gravestone. Once you were saved, once you walked with the Lord, but somehow or other, you lost it all. You do not hear the Lord anymore, nor do you see Him anymore. You are not alive to the Lord anymore.

It is the same with the church. The greatest destroyer of the church is the mindset of this world. Oh, how many times I have heard it in the gatherings of the church: "We must use common sense." What do they mean by common sense? They mean the mindset of the world. I will tell you what common sense is. If God is God, there is nothing impossible. If the Lord Jesus has been given to us as Head of the church, genuine common sense means we hear what the Head is saying. Otherwise, this other mindset destroys the church. We become affluent and complacent; in a word, Laodicean. We have the Lord's Table, we have Bible studies, we have prayer meetings, and we have evangelistic outreach. We have the whole regime, but the Lord Jesus is outside knocking, and nobody knows it. These are the most plaintive, moving words of Jesus: "If any man hear My voice and open the door, I will come in and sup with him and he with Me."

I am sure if we had members of the church of Laodicea here and asked them, "Do you believe you are overcomers?" they would say, "Yes, we know the Lord; we are saved. We have wonderful Bible teachings, the best of the bunch; they are marvellous. Really, we are a pretty alive church; I think we are overcomers." They do not even know that the Lord Jesus is outside, neither the deacons, nor the elders, none of them.

The Lord Jesus never said, "If a whole number of you will open the door ..." He came down to one person, "If any man ..." The mindset of this world, the mould of this world is the paralysis of the church. It is why every movement of the Spirit of God since Pentecost has died within generations; not one has remained alive in its original condition. They all died. It is the mindset of the world that has taken over, and it is being fashioned according to this world. Brothers and sisters, I believe this is a very serious matter.

Why does the work of the Lord become routine? The fire has gone. The apostle Paul said to Timothy, "Stir into flame the gift that is in you." Why did it die? Why does it become powerless? It is the same problem. It is the world, and it is the most seductive way Satan can use to destroy the work of God.

It is true that there are all kinds of worldly things, and we can separate ourselves from them, such as smoking. "I do not smoke. I am a believer." I was in a church once where they never went to a film, never went to theatres, never listened to an orchestra, never smoked. (Most of them did not know what tobacco smoke smelled like.) They never drank alcohol. Even at the Lord's Table there was that dreadful sacramental wine that so many believers use now, having changed the Lord's Word. It is so sad. I always wonder how the church in Corinth got drunk on that sacramental wine, but that is another matter. However, these people that I was among really believed they were separated from the world, but the real world was very much alive in them—jealousies, back-biting, unforgiving spirit, bitterness, factions, divisions, ambitions. All those things were there. You can separate from outward things of the world, and I am not saying that you should not because if the Lord speaks to you, you must obey Him. If He says, "Give up your sport," you must give it up or you will not grow because that sport can be an idol. It is the world.

"The lust of the flesh, the lust of the eyes, and the pride of life." The word *life* here is not the word that is used of eternal life or spiritual life; it is *bios* from which we get the word *biology* or *biological*. This kind of life—the lust of the flesh, the lust of the eyes, and the pride, the vain glory, the boastful pride of life, as one of the versions puts it, the natural life is the world.

Redemption for Man and the World

Do you know that when Jesus died, He laid the ground for the redemption of the natural world, the physical world? Not only did He die for human beings, but He died even for the natural creation, to redeem them from the curse, to redeem them from the emptiness and futility of their existence. We really have no idea what God originally intended with the natural creation, but what I say is biblical. We must be careful, but it is biblical. I am not asking you to go and hug trees; I am just saying that the redeeming work of the Lord Jesus extends not only to the human beings, but to the whole natural creation.

Colossians 1:19–20 says,

For it was the good pleasure of the Father that in him [Christ, Messiah] should all the fulness dwell; and through him to reconcile all things unto himself, having made peace through the blood of his cross; through him, I say, whether things upon the earth, or things in the heavens.

Romans 8:18–22 says,

> *For I reckon that the sufferings of this present time are not worthy to be compared with the glory which shall be revealed to us-ward. For the earnest expectation of the creation [the natural creation] waiteth for the revealing of the sons of God. For the creation was subjected to vanity [to futility], not of its own will, but by reason of him who subjected it, in hope that the creation itself also shall be delivered from the bondage of corruption into the liberty of the glory of the children of God. For we know that the whole creation groaneth and travaileth in pain together until now.*

So it does. For those who have ears to hear this whole natural creation groans and travails. It fell not of its own will but because of man. It waits for the fruit of the cross when the redeemed will come to that place, and then the whole natural creation will burst into life, into glory.

We often forget something that is in Revelation 4 and 5, where the little Lamb is in the throne, as if just slaughtered, and that great cry goes out: "Worthy art Thou for Thou has redeemed us with Your blood from every tongue and kindred and nation." Then myriads and myriads of angels praise Him. In chapter 5:13–14a it says, "And every created thing which is in the heaven, and on the earth, and under the earth, and on the sea, and all things that are in them, heard I saying, Unto him that sitteth on the throne, and unto the Lamb (there is the cross) be the blessing, and the honour, and the glory, and the dominion, for ever and ever. And the four living creatures (the four living ones) said, "Amen."

A New Creation

I do not know how many of you have ever thought about the cherubim. They are found in Ezekiel, wheels within wheels. They go up, down, sideways, backwards, forwards. If you look on the outward it is man, and on one side it is an ox; look the other side it is a lion; look inside it is an eagle. They are the same living creatures that are around the throne in Revelation 4 and 5, but they are not angels. Seraphim are angels; cherubim are not angels. What are they? I always remember Mr. Sparks saying that he thought and thought and puzzled and puzzled over the cherubim. He said the one thing they are not is those little chubby babies that you see with little wings. But he said, and I think he followed G.H. Pember in this, "It is the whole creation—the animal creation, the bird creation, the domestic animals, the wild animals, and man as well—redeemed by the grace of God. Here is something wonderful, "a new heaven and a new earth wherein dwells righteousness." The demonic principle of sin has gone, and in its place is righteousness. It is wonderful!

Man has been gloriously saved by the work of Christ crucified. The cross is the way to glory. In Ephesians it speaks about walking according to the course of this world, according to the power of the air, the spirit that now dwells in the sons of disobedience, and there was no hope for us. But God!—being rich in mercy made us alive together with Christ. How did He make us alive? Through the work of the cross. He took the old man and crucified him, and He took the old creation and crucified it. It is a new creation, a new man in the Messiah (see Ephesians 2). It is so wonderful;

it is the work of the cross and the redemption. This new man is now Christ-centred, Christ-conscious, and Christ-dependent.

Galatians 6:14 says, "But far be it from me to glory, save in the cross of our Lord Jesus the Messiah, through which the world hath been crucified unto me, and I unto the world."

This is the only way that you can give the Lord Jesus the pre-eminence in your life and in your service, the only way that He can be the living, functional, practical Head of the church, the only way you can serve God. It is the only way the mindset of the world can be broken, the mould of this age broken, our minds renewed and thus transformed to prove what is the good and acceptable and perfect will of God.

Let me finish by asking a question. If you are a leader, if you are responsible for other lives, is the world crucified to you and you to the world? Dear child of God, you young person, is the world crucified to you and you to the world? You are playing with the wrong kind of fire if you are playing with the world. It will corrupt you, seduce you, and destroy you. Listen to me!
Shall we pray:

Beloved Lord, touch our hearts. Don't let us be the same people who are just sermon tasting. Deliver us from academic knowledge. Lord, face us; don't let us escape. We want to go on into all Your purpose in these days. We want to see Your eternal purpose fulfilled, and we want to pray that we will be involved in the fulfilment. If it means we must lose our self-life, as it does, may Your Holy Spirit energize us to let go of that self-life. Hear us, Lord. We ask it in the name of our Lord Jesus. Amen.

5. What is Worldliness?

Galatians 6:14
But far be it from me to glory, save in the cross of our Lord Jesus Christ, through which the world hath been crucified unto me, and I unto the world.

John 12:31
Now is the judgment of this world: now shall the prince of this world be cast out.

1 John 5:19
We know that we are of God, and the whole world lieth in the evil one.

Ephesians 6:10–13
Finally, be strong in the Lord and in the strength of His might. Put on the whole armour of God, that ye may be able to stand against the wiles of the devil. For our wrestling is not against flesh and blood, but against the principalities, against the powers, against the world rulers of this darkness, against hosts of wicked spirits in the heavens. Wherefore, take up the full armour of God, that ye may be able to withstand the evil day, and having done all to stand.

> **1 John 2:15–17**
> *Love not the world, neither the things that are in the world. If any man love the world, the love of the Father is not in him. For all that is in the world, the lust of the flesh and the lust of the eyes and the vainglory of life, is not of the Father, but is of the world. And the world passeth away, and the lust thereof: but he that doeth the will of God abideth for ever.*

Just a further word of prayer:

Dear beloved Lord, we are so thankful that we are here found in Your presence. And Lord, we just want to recognize now before You, that without You, we can do nothing of eternal worth. We can speak many words, outline truths, it can even be sound doctrine, but unless that anointing of Yours is upon us in full measure, it will all amount to nothing. Lord, You have provided us with such an anointing, both for the speaking of Your Word, the translating of Your Word, and the hearing of Your Word. Into that anointing grace and power we now stand in simple faith. Let a double portion of that anointing be upon us all, and may we thus meet with You and may something happen in our lives that is eternal. We ask it in the name of our Messiah, the Lord Jesus. Amen.

I want to ask a question and then by the grace of God answer it. What is worldliness? The greatest disease among believers is worldliness, because it paralyses and infects spiritual health.

It causes those who could grow up to be strong in the Lord to be weak; more than weak, they sometimes become tools of the adversary of God. Paul says that the world has been crucified to me, and I to the world through the cross of Christ. What is worldliness? What is a worldly Christian? Worldliness is the love of this world; not just love for the sinner but love for the world. A worldly child of God is basically in love with this world. John put it so simply: "Love not the world, neither the things that are within it. He that loves the world, the love of the Father is not in him."

James says in his own severe way, "Ye adulteresses, know you not that friendship with the world is hostility to God?" Worldliness is to be in a state of hostility with God. He says, "Whosoever therefore would be a friend of the world is an enemy of God." This is a severe truth and it comes to us in an uncomfortable way. But it is absolute truth. You cannot be in love with this world and in love with the Lord Jesus. The love of the Father cannot be in us if we love the world and the things that are within it. It is a question of our commitment to the Lord. The basic, essential spirit of the world is put very simply, as always, by John: "The lust of the flesh, the lust of the eyes, and the boastful pride of physical life." That is the basic, essential spirit of this world.

When God first created this world and everything within it, it was good. But with the fall of Satan, with the fall of a third of the angels, and with the fall of man, something entered into this world so that now Satan is called the prince of this world. This title is nowhere contested in the Word of God. The ruler of this world, the prince of this world is Satan himself. John puts it again in his own simple, clear, black and white manner: "We know that we are of God and the whole world lies in the evil one." What then is this Trojan horse that is within the believer? What is it in the believer that hinders him from being joined to the Lord, wedded to the Lord, and causes him or her to be wedded to this world?

Very often we think there is nothing wrong in the world. I am saved and converted; I have been born of God. Surely I can handle the world. We are not talking about handling the world; we are talking about being wedded to the world. That is why James says, "You adulteresses, you who have been called to be married to the Lord Jesus are giving yourself to another." It is a serious matter. It involves demons. It involves evil spirits. It involves world rulers of this darkness. It involves principalities and powers that are spiritual. This is no fairy tale; it is absolute truth. That is why so many works, so-called of God, are paralysed. It is why so much of the church is paralysed and has become a community like any other human community. It is not the body of the Lord Jesus. It is not wedded to a heaven at the right hand of God. It is not manifesting all the power and glory of the Lord Jesus, but instead it is so often a nest for evil, for hypocrisy, for division, for faction, for jealousy, for ambition. It all goes back to worldliness.

We often think of worldliness as the outward things, such as alcohol, smoking, the way you dress, television, newspapers, novels, and I could go on and on. Those things are symptoms, but it is not essential worldliness.

The Character of the World

Romans 1:29–32 says,

> *Being filled with all unrighteousness, wickedness, covetousness, maliciousness; full of envy, murder, strife, deceit, malignity; whisperers, back-biters, hateful to God, insolent, haughty, boastful, inventors of evil things, disobedient to parents, without understanding, covenant-breakers, without natural affection, unmerciful: who, knowing the ordinance of God, that they that practise such things are worthy of death, not only do the same, but also consent with them that practise them.*

This is the divine description of this world and the essential character of this world. So we should not be surprised. It bears and expresses the character of Satan and those angels that fell with him which became the basic character of this world. As we look at the history of this world we find that it is full of these things on the grandest scale and the most minute scale, from great empires and ideologies that have bound millions of human beings, to the family and the individual human being who lives like this. But someone will say, "Brother, why are you talking to us about these things? You are describing an unsaved world, and we are believers. Surely, you are not describing us."

The World in the Church

Colossians 3:5–10 says,

> *Speaking of the cross and the world, "Put to death therefore your members which are upon the earth: fornication, [immorality], uncleanness, [pornography], passion, evil desire, and covetousness, which is idolatry; for which things' sake cometh the wrath of God upon the sons of disobedience: wherein ye also once walked, when ye lived in these things; but now do ye also put them all away: anger, wrath, malice, railing, shameful speaking out of your mouth: lie not one to another; seeing that ye have put off the old man with his doings, and have put on the new man, that is being renewed unto knowledge after the image of him that created him.*

The apostle was speaking to born-again believers, to a living, born-again church. We would say that for many of us these things he is describing have nothing whatsoever to do with a child of God nor with the church of God nor with the work of the gospel. But I am old enough to have seen it all. So much of Christian life is a façade for the world, but behind the façade there is jealousy, back-biting, faction, unrivalled ambition, all these things.

James 3:13–16 says,

> *"Who is wise and understanding among you? Let him show by his good life his works in meekness of wisdom. But if ye have bitter jealousy and faction in your heart, glory not and lie not against the truth. This wisdom*

is not a wisdom that cometh down from above, but is earthly, sensual, devilish. For where jealousy and faction are, there is confusion and every vile deed."

This is spoken to believers, to a real church. It is spoken to those who are workers in God's gospel. It is something that you and I need to face.

What is worldliness? Worldliness, essentially, is the lust of the flesh, the lust of the eyes, and the boastful pride of physical life. Where there is no dealing with that, it will not be long before these things begin to be found in our lives and amongst us. You cannot play with fire and not be burnt. It is that simple. Sometimes when you are young, you think you will only be young once, so you kick down the rails and enjoy yourself. But there is a terrible enemy and he will bind you and lead you along a path so gently that you do not even know it is the power of darkness. However, the end is bondage, paralysis, hypocrisy, Christian façade, and behind it the world.

If reading a newspaper is worldly, I am very worldly. I once went to a group not very far from here to speak at a little retreat they had, and they did not even know that Robert Kennedy had been assassinated in Los Angeles. They did not listen to the radio nor did they have a television. They were separated from the world, but the world was in them. I am not making any appeal for you to become big newspaper readers; I would rather you read the Bible; study the Bible. I am not asking you to be watchers of televisions; better be watchmen on the walls of Jerusalem. No, I am not asking for that, but these things are only symptoms of worldliness. Real worldliness is the problem.

When I was first saved, I was in a fellowship that was very separated from the world. You had to be dressed just right. Boys could not wear shirts opened to the waist. The girls could not wear little skirts that were only about a foot from the waist. We all had to dress in a special way. We were not allowed to go to the movies. We were not allowed to go to the theatre. We were not permitted to listen to orchestral music. We were not allowed to go to sports, such as football games, although for some strange reason, they thought tennis was spiritual. There was no alcohol, no smoking, and no make-up. When a lady came in with lipstick on, all the heads would turn to look at her. The pastor called them post boxes because in Britain the post boxes are painted red. That was the kind of group my sister and I landed in. They were wonderful people, loved the Lord, sang the hymns from their heart, but you have no idea of the worldliness that was there. This was a Baptist Church and in their church meetings people called each other names and lost their tempers with each other. I have never forgotten it. The bottom of my Christian life fell out by watching those older people. Here I was separated from the world and watching the world at work.

What is worldliness? It is the essential spirit of this world, and the seriousness of worldliness for a believer is that he or she makes themselves available to evil spirits and demons. You cannot play with fire and not be burnt.

The Cross Deals with the World

What did the apostle mean when he said, "Put to death, therefore your members which are upon the earth"? Surely he meant that the world has to be dealt with through the cross. In the Greek, you can say *through whom*. "Far be it from me to glory, save in the Lord Jesus, the Messiah, through whom the world is crucified to me and I to the world."

What am I to do? You can try to crucify yourself, but you will have a very, very difficult time. I tried to do it for some years. Think! How do you crucify yourself? You have a hammer and you have a nail, and first of all, start with the feet. You bend down, and you bang the nail through your feet. Then you take a nail and hammer it into one hand, but what about the other one? You cannot crucify yourself. Try! Then it becomes religion and heaviness and darkness. There is no life in it; there is no resurrection life resulting. It is just religion, Christian religion.

In Christ

The apostle Paul says in Galatians 2:20, "I have been crucified with Christ. Nevertheless, I live, yet not I, but Christ liveth in me. And the life which I now live, I live by the faith of the Son of God, who loved me and gave Himself for me."

You will notice that it is all to do with life—spiritual life, eternal life, resurrection life. Everyone puts the accent on being crucified with Christ, but listen: "I have been crucified with Christ; nevertheless, I live, yet not I, but Christ liveth in me." We are under new management. It is as simple as that; we are under new management. "I have been crucified with Christ; nevertheless, I live, yet not I, but Christ liveth in me. And the life which I now live, I live by the faith of the Son of God, who loved me and gave Himself for me."

What a gospel! It is life—abundant life, overflowing life, resurrection life, the power of life, and it all stems from this, "I have been crucified with Christ." Do you sometimes think to yourself, "I must be crucified"? You will never be crucified—not that way. It will end in religion, the affliction of the flesh, will-worship; it is not the way.

Let me illustrate it this way which is the best way I have ever heard it illustrated. Here is a Bible and here is a marker. This Bible is Christ and the marker is you. Now God knew that you would be saved, and in His foreknowledge He took you and put you in Christ. You cannot see the marker when it is in the Bible; you can only see the Bible. God sees you in Christ; He put you in Christ. If I put the Bible on a table, where is the marker? The marker is in the Bible, so the marker is on the table. Now if I take the Bible and put it on the piano the marker is still in the Bible. You cannot see it, but it is in the Bible. The history of the Bible is the history of the marker. The Bible was on the table, and the marker was on the table. The Bible was on the piano, and the marker was on the piano.

God put you in Christ; therefore, when Christ was crucified, you were crucified. It is a historic fact. It does not matter what you feel. When Christ died, you died. He not only died for you, He died as you. You cannot put to death the members of your body on the earth unless you first know that He died, and when He died, you died. You cannot deal with worldliness by just trying to come at it head on; you can only deal with it through Christ. That is why the Word of God says, "By the Spirit, put to death the deeds of the body." It is impossible to know the death of Christ apart from the Holy Spirit. It is the Holy Spirit who enlightens your mind, who reveals the truth, who illuminates you so that you suddenly see when Christ died, you died. Then you can reckon on it. It is not make believe.

I used to know a dear, dear brother who would always pinch himself. Then he would feel it and say, "Ahhh, I have been crucified with Christ." But knowing the way he lived I became very suspicious. It seemed to me as if it was mind over matter—Christian Science. If you have a headache, you say, "I *do not* have a headache, I do not have a headache, I do not have a headache, I *definitely* do not have a headache." Psychologically it works, but it is not the faith which is the gift of God. Faith, which is the gift of God, means you reckon on eternal facts. Now you can reckon yourself dead indeed to sin when you see that when Christ died, you died.

Giving up All Right to Self

There is another wonderful Scripture in Mark's gospel 8:34a: "If any man follow me, let him deny himself and take up his cross, and follow me." Mark this carefully: "follow—follow. If any man follow me, let him follow." What comes in between? "If any man follow me, let him deny himself." That is the core of worldliness. Let me put it another way: let him give up all right to himself. The whole problem is rights; "I have rights." In fact you mean that your self-life has rights.

We are living in a world of rights. There are women's rights, the unborn's rights, trees' rights, animal rights, fishes' rights; everything has rights, except men. Nobody ever talks about men's rights. It is all women's rights, hugging trees, all about the ecology—rights, rights, rights, rights. Rights are the deepest instinct in us. "I will *not* have anybody step on me. I will *not* allow myself to be limited, curtailed, overlooked. My self-life has rights. I have ambition, and I have a right to climb the ladder." "If any man follow me …" This is the most basic step; let him give up all right to himself and take up his cross.

These pictures we see in Ecclesiastical structures of Jesus bearing a cross are quite wrong because the upright of the cross was always in place at the place of execution. Sometimes it was the trunk of a tree, sometimes a living tree, sometimes a dead tree, but the upright was always there. The disciples and the multitudes that Jesus called together to hear this had all seen this a thousand times. The soldiers would be there clearing the way and shouting, "Out of the way; out of the way!" Behind them would come the prisoner with a card hanging around his neck with the sentence of death and the reason for his death written on it. He would be carrying the cross beam on his way to the execution ground.

First, you must understand that when Christ died, you died. You cannot crucify yourself, but you can give up all right to yourself. That is the most basic step that you can take, and only the Holy Spirit can enable you to take that step because the deepest instinct in man is self-preservation. You can give up all right to yourself and take up your cross beam. Now you understand what the apostle Paul meant when he said, "We have the sentence of death within ourselves, that we should not trust in ourselves, but in God who raises the dead" (see II Corinthians 1:9).

God Arranges the Circumstances

You are on the way to the execution but you cannot crucify yourself. So how are you crucified? You are crucified in Christ, but in practical terms, how does it happen? You do not have to worry about that; God takes care of the execution. Your nearest and dearest will do it for you. Your husband will do the job. Your wife will do the job. Your parents will do the job. Your children will do the job. Your employer will do the job. Your employees will certainly do the job. If none of those do it, be sure the church will do it. You cannot get away. Give up all right to yourself, take up your cross beam, accept the sentence of death, and God will arrange the circumstances and situations.

People sometimes say, "Why did this happen to me? Why is so and so this difficult?" Instead they should be saying, "Praise the Lord; this is an opportunity to die." I mean it. It is not just a joke; it is an opportunity to die. I have heard people say sometimes, "Lord, help me to be crucified. Help me to fall into the ground and die." But when the Lord arranges the circumstances, they are really upset.

Worldliness! You may think, young person, that it is no big deal to get involved with the world, but in your innocence, you have no idea of the spiritual powers that are hovering around you to bind you, and to destroy you. This worldliness will destroy you. It will destroy the church and it will destroy our service for God. We can begin in the spirit and end in the flesh. What was once alive to God—hearing the Lord, seeing the Lord, following the Lord—is now lifeless, a monument. It all goes back to this simple matter. In II Corinthians 4:10 Paul says this: "Always bearing about in the body the dying of Jesus, that the life also of Jesus may be manifested in our mortal body." This is the only antidote to worldliness.

Where do you stand in this matter? Have you deliberately given up all right to yourself? Are you taking up your cross beam? You cannot follow Him in any other way. I can only say that I am so thankful that in the early days of my Christian life, I came to this decision. It cost me very much because in the church I was in the pastor had made all the arrangements for me to go to Bible College (thank God I never went), one that was very well known and he had it all planned out. But because I had given up all right to myself, I had another Master. I asked Him what I should do, and He said, "Do not go this way, and I will take care of you." I can testify that He has. I can never say the Lord is in my debt, that He is indebted to me: "I gave up everything for Him and now He must do a lot for me. I gave up all this path, the ladder to go up and up and up." The pastor even said, "In the end you will be a Keswick speaker." I was young, only a kid of 18 or 19 years old, but I let it all go and the Lord has been to me so much that I am continuously in His debt.

Dear child of God, there is nothing in this world like following the Lord Jesus, but you cannot follow Him if He is not Lord. You cannot follow Him if you do not give up all right to yourself. You cannot follow Him if you are not prepared to die daily. May the Lord touch our hearts. There is so much of the world in all of us, me included, and we must remember this word: "To put to death our members that are on the earth." But with the fulness that comes, the resurrection life that comes, the joy that comes, the laughter that fills our mouths, the sense of purpose, who is going to talk about dying? It is the pathway to the fulfilment of the eternal purpose of God.

Let's pray:

Beloved Lord, we are such poor material; we have to confess it. We love the world and the things that are in it. We get so involved, Lord; not only on the outward level but often in its basic, essential spirit. Forgive us, cleanse us, and bring us to the place where we will be able to say with the apostle Paul, "Far be it from me to glory, save in the Lord Jesus, the Messiah, through whom the world has been crucified to me, and I to the world." We ask it all in the name of our Lord Jesus. Amen.

6.
A Living Sacrifice

Galatians 6:14
But far be it from me to glory, save in the cross of our Lord Jesus Christ, through which the world has been crucified unto me, and I unto the world.

Romans 12:1–8
I beseech you, therefore brethren, by the mercies of God, to present your bodies a living sacrifice, holy, acceptable to God, which is your spiritually intelligent worship and service. And be not fashioned according to this world: but be ye transformed by the renewing of your mind, that ye may prove what is the good and acceptable and perfect will of God. For I say, through the grace that was given me, to every man that is among you, not to think of himself more highly than he ought to think; but so to think as to think soberly, according as God hath dealt to each man a measure of faith. For even as we have many members in one body, and all the members have not the same office: so we,

who are many, are one body in Christ, and severally members one of another. And having gifts differing according to the grace that was given to us, whether prophecy, let us prophesy according to the proportion of our faith; or ministry, let us give ourselves to our ministry; or he that teacheth, to his teaching; or he that exhorteth, to his exhorting: he that giveth, let him do it with liberality; he that ruleth, with diligence; he that showeth mercy, with cheerfulness.

Colossians 1:12–15
Giving thanks unto the Father, who made us meet to be partakers of the inheritance of the saints in light; who delivered us out of the power of darkness, and translated us into the kingdom of the Son of his love; in whom we have our redemption, the forgiveness of our sins: who is the image of the invisible God, the firstborn of all creation.

Just a further word of prayer:

Beloved Lord, You are present amongst us. We are gathering to You, and we want just to recognize that without You we can do nothing of eternal worth. You have provided us with an anointing, and we dare not ignore it. Lord, by faith, we stand into that anointing grace and power for the speaking of Your Word, for the translating of Your Word, and for the hearing of Your Word. Touch our hearts and challenge us, Lord. Don't let us escape from this matter. Corner us by Your Holy Spirit and follow us until You get us. Hear us, Lord, and we shall be careful to give You all the thanksgiving of our hearts. We ask this in the name of our Messiah, the Lord Jesus. Amen.

John, the apostle, said, "Love not the world neither the things that are within it." And I have sought to explain that there are two different Greek words translated in English by the same word, *world*. One is *cosmos*, which is the whole universe and everything within it—all the beauty and all the inhabitants that are within it. The other word is *eon*. It speaks of an age, the course and duration of time. Both these words on the whole have an unfavorable meaning in the Word of God.

We have spoken about this world that God created of which He said, "It is good." But with the fall of Satan and a third of the angels, followed by the fall of man, something entered into this world that was never there before—the poison of the snake. It has infected the whole of this world and the ages of time. For this reason Satan is called the prince of this world. In the temptation of the Messiah, Satan came to Him and said, "Bow down and worship me and I will give you *all* the nations and their glory," Jesus never said to Him, "You lie." All He said was "You shall worship the Lord your God and Him only shall you serve." John, the apostle, puts it very simply in 1 John 5:19. "We (believers) know that we are of God, and the whole world (*cosmos*) lieth in the evil one." This is the same word we have in Galatians 6:14: "Far be it from me to glory, save in our Lord Jesus the Messiah, through whom the world has been crucified unto me, and I unto the world."

Next we asked the question: "What is worldliness?" Many people think worldliness is things you dress in, things you look at, things you do, but worldliness in its heart is the lust of the flesh, the lust of the eyes, and the vain glory of life, physical life. We could speak endlessly about the world. It extends over everything from commerce, to money, to property, to pride, to jealousy, to ambition; it goes on and on and on.

There is no answer at all to worldliness except the cross. It is God's one and only way of dealing with it. It is through Christ crucified that worldliness is dealt with. How can Christ live in you and you be worldly? How can Christ crucified dwell in the believer and that believer be in love with this world? John puts it so simply. "He that loveth the world, the love of the Father is not in him." That means all our talk about loving the Lord is a sham. James even more severely says, "You adulteresses, do you not know that friendship with the world is hostility to God? He that would be a friend of the world is an enemy of God." This is very black and white. There is no mixture, no in between.

The Roman letter is the greatest exposition of the gospel in the sixty-six books of the Bible. As the apostle Paul begins to sum up everything in chapter 12 he says, "I beseech you therefore, brethren ..." in light of all these eleven chapters. "I beseech you therefore, brethren, by the mercies of God, to present your bodies a living sacrifice." That is the cross in action. The practical outcome of being crucified with Christ is to become a living sacrifice. He could have said, "I beseech you therefore, brethren, by the mercies of God, that you study the gospel." This could have been a very academic exercise. He could have said, "I beseech you therefore, brethren, by the mercies of God, that you be devoted in your service." Instead he said, "I beseech you, therefore brethren, by the mercies of God to present your bodies a living sacrifice." I beseech you therefore, brethren, by the mercies of God, to present your bodies a burnt offering—not just consecrated, but to go up in smoke. Burnt! A burnt offering! Nothing else is acceptable to God!

Do you want to be set apart? Do you want to be holy? You must be a living sacrifice. Do you want to be well-pleasing to God, acceptable to God? You must be a living sacrifice. There is no alternative. This is the interim goal of the gospel. The ultimate goal of the gospel is the bride. But if you have been saved, if you have been washed in the blood of the Lamb, if you have been justified in the sight of God through the finished work of the Messiah, then you must present your bodies a living sacrifice. There is no other way.

Sometimes, we hear it said in Christian circles that we should consecrate our talents, that we should dedicate our natural gifts. "Have you a gift of the gab? (That is an Irish saying.) Dedicate it to the Lord and you will be a preacher. Have you got the gift for music? Dedicate it to the Lord and you will be a worship leader. Have you got the gift of organizing? Consecrate it to the Lord and He will use it to develop order out of the mess in the church." But what the Lord demands is a living sacrifice. That means your body, your personality, your talents, your gifts, your energy, your whole being; everything you are is to be a living sacrifice.

Spiritually Intelligent Worship

It is interesting to note this little word: "which is your spiritually intelligent worship and service." Some translations say "your rational or reasonable service," but that does not convey the real spiritual meaning. Sometimes worship has very much emotion in it. That is not wrong. It is strange if you were to worship the Lord like a machine. Of course there is emotion. Rightly, there should be emotion. And, of course, there is emotion in service. Often we give ourselves to the Lord in a moment of real emotion. In a meeting like this, we are stirred not only in our spirit, but in our emotion and will. What then does this extraordinary phrase mean?

"I beseech you therefore, brethren, by the mercies of God, to present your bodies a living sacrifice, holy, acceptable to God, which is your spiritually intelligent worship and service." It is not just your reason or emotion; it is spiritual intelligence. Let me put it another way. It means that in a cold-blooded and deliberate way you have decided to present your body a living sacrifice. *That* is real worship; not the emotion of a moment or something reasoned out in a moment. It is a deliberate, determined act of worship, your spiritually intelligent worship and service.

There is no alternative to being a living sacrifice, and Satan knows it. He knows it so well that he will fight to keep any believer from being a living sacrifice. He will entice you, he will seduce you, he will get you into bondage like a spider's web. He will weave it all around you until you cannot move. It is like an octopus with eight arms; once you have gotten rid of one, you still have the other seven. So is Satan's strategy. He knows that when believers become a living sacrifice, nothing is impossible. They will go on to prove what is the good, acceptable, and perfect will of God. If you are not a living sacrifice, you will never know that. He knows that the mold of this world, the straitjacket of this world, the fashion of this world will never be broken apart from being a living sacrifice. You can study the Bible, you can sing the hymns, you can attend the meetings, but that straitjacket of the world, the world's mold you are in, is still there. It is a mindset.

The Fashion of the World

"And be not fashioned [molded] according to this age, but be ye transformed by the renewing of your mind." When your mind is renewed, you are transformed and you are out of bondage. The octopus is dead and the web has gone. You are ready to fly into the heavens. It is a living sacrifice. It is only when you become a living sacrifice that the mindset of this age and the world is broken. Then you can be free to have the mind of Christ and become a bondslave. Then you can humble yourself so that He can exalt you. It all goes back to being a living sacrifice.

What is the curse of the church? It is the fashion of this world and the mindset of this world. We make the church just like any other human organization. It has its membership role; it has its members; it has its election procedures; it has its organization, just like any other human club, and it destroys the church. In that early church, before the Holy Spirit came, there were one hundred and twenty units of a congregation. After the Holy Spirit came, there were one hundred and twenty members of the body of Christ. They were joined to the Head at the right hand of God, and when He was manifested by the Holy Spirit, the whole Jewish world was turned upside down. In the end the Greek and the Roman world were turned upside down and inside out. It did not have the organization that we have today, but the simple union with the Head by the Spirit of God meant that it was invincible. Such is the wonder of being a living sacrifice.

The world's mold is broken and the world's mindset is broken to be transformed. If only every member of the body of Christ was being transformed! Can you imagine the effect upon the world? But it is not only proving what is the good and acceptable and perfect will of God, being a living sacrifice leads to an expression of the one body in Christ. Notice that it is not one body *of* Christ; it is one body *in* Christ, and individually members one of another. When we are not a living sacrifice, we may have the Bible in our heads, we may have a lot of zeal, we may have a lot of other things, but we always remain individuals preserving our individual entity.

How well I remember when I first saw what the church is, that it is Christ, and it blew my mind away. That moment I ceased to be a Baptist and became a member of the body of Christ. In that moment, every child of God belonged to me and I belonged to them. But when I went back into the church I was in, I suddenly realized that I was like a fish out of water; we were all individuals. No one seemed to feel that they belonged to you. I did not know anything about the people I had known for years. The body of Christ is an amazing thing. You cannot set it up; it has to be born of God, and you have to have a nucleus of believers who are all living sacrifices. When you have that nucleus, the church begins to be expressed. It is not just a doctrine in our head; that is deadness and it leads to pride: "We are the church; you are not. We understand these things, you do not. We are superior, you are inferior. We are elite, you are common." But when you are a living sacrifice, you will serve every child of God in this universe. You will not be a partaker of their sins, but you will love them and serve them. Inwardly, you belong to them and they belong to you, and you cannot overcome this.

Natural Gifts

"Having gifts differing" (Romans 12:6). There are natural gifts such as a person who has the gift of the gab. They can preach but you are bored stiff. They have the natural talent, but nothing touches your spirit. There is another person who can play, and when you hear their playing, you think, "Good," or "not so good," but you are left with them. Another person plays and it is a ministry of Christ. What is the difference? Why can one person speak and it is a ministry of Christ, and another person speaks and it is just words? Sometimes they are even brilliant words, but they are only words. One person sings, and it is a good voice; another person sings and you are in the presence of the Lord. One person can organize, but they organize the Holy Spirit right out of the church. It has happened again and again in the history of the church. Another person organizes and it is the Lord. What is the key? The key is to be a living sacrifice. Then it is not self-expression, self-aggrandizement, self-fulfillment; it is a ministry of Christ.

I think it is amazing that the apostle Paul concludes with this. Of course he is like so many of us writers and preachers; he goes on for another four chapters. But here was the beginning of the conclusion: "I beseech you therefore, brethren, by the mercies of God, to present your bodies a living sacrifice, holy, acceptable unto God, which is your spiritually intelligent worship and service." Have you ever presented your body? Are you ready to be a living sacrifice?

The Fact and Challenge of the Cross

The other matter that is much on my heart is the fact of the cross and the challenge. Let me go back again to Galatians 6:14: "Far be it from me to glory, save in the Lord Jesus, the Messiah, through whom the world has been crucified unto me, and I unto the world." It is an historic fact that when Christ was crucified, I was crucified, and you were crucified whether you knew it or not. Secondly, our old man was crucified; "the man of old" is a good way to put it, isn't it? The man of old was crucified; it is an historic fact. The world was crucified with Christ. That is why there will be a new heaven and a new earth wherein dwells righteousness. That is why there will be a universe out of which the whole poison of the snake has been drawn. There will be no more curse, no more dying, no more mourning, no more death; it is all passed away. It is a fact, and we cannot deal with worldliness in our being in any other way.

Do not be Entangled Again

What is the challenge of this to us? First of all, Colossians 1:13: "Who delivered us out of the power or domain of darkness, and translated us into the kingdom of His Son." Here is the first challenge. Do not be entangled again with the yoke of bondage. Do not let Satan seduce you. It may seem so good to begin with, so innocuous, but you will come into a terrible bondage. It can be in business, in your work life and professional life, in your family, in your individual life, in church life. It can be as those who are serving the Lord, which should be all of us. Do not be entangled again.

God delivered you and delivered me out of the authority of darkness at tremendous cost. Satan and his hosts had authority over you and over me. We were blind, helpless, and bound. Then, through the finished work of the Lord Jesus, when He was made my sin and your sin, when He bore the punishment of our sin in His own body, when it pleased the Lord to crush Him, you were miraculously delivered out of the authority of darkness. You could not do it. No church nor any religious organization could do it. Only God could do it. But it is more than that.

He not only delivered you, freed you, broke the fetters, and delivered you from the authority of darkness, but He transferred you into the kingdom of His dear Son. Here is the first challenge. Are you bound? Are you playing with darkness? Are you compromising with this world, whether in business, in the making of money, in your family, in your relationships, in your self as a person, in the church, in the service of God? You cannot play with darkness and have it not enter you. You cannot play with fire and not be burnt. You cannot ride on the tiger and not be eaten. You have been made free by Christ; do not be entangled again in a yoke of bondage. Why is it a yoke of bondage? Because when the yoke is on, you can steer the animal.

Submit to His Lordship

Here is the second challenge. If you have been transferred into the kingdom of God's beloved Son, there is a King and there is a Lord. The challenge is this: submit to His Lordship. Luke 6:46

says, "And why call ye me, Lord, Lord, and do not the things which I say?" Good question. "Why do you call me Lord, and you do not do what I say?" I will tell you why; you are not a living sacrifice. You cannot get out of that mold; it is still there.

Many, many times I have used the words of the mother of Jesus to those who have just come to the Lord, words she spoke at the wedding in Cana. She said to the servants, "Whatsoever He says, do it." This is the simple key to the Christian life. This is the simple key to following the Lord. "Whatsoever He says, do it." If He says to you, "Give up this friendship," give it up. The Lord may give it back to you at some point, but if He says it, do it. If there is some worldliness and He says, "Give it up;" give it up."

I remember a sister who came one day to the morning meeting. This dear girl, who was a waitress and could only come in the morning, had no Christian background whatsoever. As she watched the bread being broken and the cup being poured at the Lord's Table, she saw the Lord. The person doing it disappeared, and she saw the Lord. She was saved. She hardly knew what salvation was, but she got saved. She came to see me, and I said to her, "The key to your Christian life is whatsoever the Lord says, do it. Do you have any problem with that?"

"No, no, no. I will do it." Then she turned to go out from the study and suddenly she turned around and said, "There is one thing; I am not taking this lipstick off."

And I said, "Who spoke about lipstick? Was there anything in the Lord's Table about lipstick?"

"No, no, no," she said, "no one said anything. But I noticed that all those sisters did not have any powder or rouge on their face, and no lipstick on their lips. I do not want to be a dying swan. I am very pale. I have blonde hair and pale skin."

"Look," I said, "why are you caught on this matter? Nobody has talked about it. Nobody told you that you must take it all off. You are saved, and you are a child of God; you can have it." I could see she did not believe me, so I said, "Listen, you make a promise to me. You promise that you will never take off your make-up unless the Lord speaks to you."

"All right," she said. "that is a deal." And out she went.

For about six to nine months she wore the make-up. Then one day, I noticed there was no make-up. So I went straight over and said, "What about the deal we made?"

"What do you mean?" she said.

I said, "We made a deal about the make-up. You promised you would never take it off unless the Lord spoke to you. Are you trying to be one with all the others?"

"No," she said, "the Lord spoke to me."

Then, I said, "You have done the right thing."

So it is with sports or with a thousand and one other things. If the Lord speaks to you, obey Him. "Trust and obey for there's no other way to be happy in Jesus, but to trust and obey." I can tell you that sometimes the Lord gives you back things. He takes them away, and He gives them back.

When I was a little boy of three or four years of age, I loved scissors. My desire in life was to get hold of a pair of scissors. My mother thought I would be a tailor because so many Jews are tailors. I loved shears, big scissors, all of them, and my mother spent a lot of time running around saying, "Give me those scissors." And I would say, "Never!" I hugged them to myself, and in the end, mother had to pull them away from me. Then I would have a tantrum, and I thought to myself, my mother is a witch. She takes away the things I like. I understand now that I have grown up why she had to take those scissors away. They would have damaged me. When the Lord tells you to give something up, it is because He loves you, not because He wants to give you a bad time. He says, "Give that to me. You do not realize it will damage you." But some things He will give back. Here is the challenge: Obey the King. You have been transferred into the kingdom of God's beloved Son; obey Him.

A Steward—Not an Owner

The third thing is to learn that you are a steward, not an owner. That means you are not your own; you are bought with a price. Therefore, glorify God in your body.

> *Or know ye not that your body is a temple of the Holy Spirit which is in you, which ye have from God? and ye are not your own; for ye were bought with a price: glorify God therefore in your body. (1 Corinthians 6:19–20)*

> *According as each man hath received a gift, ministering it among yourselves, as good stewards of the manifold grace of God. (1 Peter 4:10)*

> *And the multitude of them that believed were of one heart and soul: and not one of them said that ought of the things which he possessed was his own; but they had all things common. (Acts 4:32)*

When you are a living sacrifice, you are no longer an owner; you are a steward. There is a vast difference between an owner and a steward. When you are an owner, you are the authority. When you are a steward, you are under authority. You should be the steward of everything you own, not the owner of it. When you are not a living sacrifice, this kind of talk is very hard to hear. "You mean my home? I should share it?" Yes, at times. "You mean my car? I should share it? Oh no, not here in America." I notice everywhere cars with one person in them. You even have HOV lanes for the cars with two or more people, and there are not so many in these lanes, I notice. I thank God for those HOV lanes because I am always in a car with two or three others. Everything you own is not what you own, not when you belong to the Lord. You are a steward of it and you will have to give an account of your stewardship.

I came to the Lord through an extraordinary man. His name was C.T. Studd, an amazing missionary. He went with the Cambridge Seven to China first, and when he went to have his medical, the doctor said, "You cannot go; you are a museum of diseases." But C.T. Studd said, "Someone with greater authority than you, Doctor, has told me to go, and I am going with a museum of diseases."

C.T. Studd was a famous cricketer, one of the really great cricketers of history. When he came to the Lord, he had a fortune. Today it would be millions and millions of dollars. In one week, he gave it all away, every penny of it. He had to trust for his fare to China. Why did he give it away? Because the Lord told him to, and out of that obedience, thousands upon thousands throughout the world have come to know the Lord Jesus, and I am one of them. C.T. Studd was a strange old man, full of weaknesses and faults, but he was for me the illustration of a thorn bush with the fire of God in it. You met the Lord in him, and you heard the Lord through him. Why did the Lord tell him to give up all his fortune? Could he not have used it? But in the wisdom of God, the Lord knew that if he held onto his fortune, it would have destroyed him. He could never have been what God wanted him to be if he had held onto that fortune.

I knew another person who was a titled lady. She was twenty years of age when she married. She had a title from her own father, and she married a military man who also had a title. Three years after they were married, he died in the Spanish flu epidemic. (It is the same type of thing that everybody today is afraid of with bird flu.) So there she was as a child of God without her husband who was only a few years older than her, and she had an enormous fortune. She said to me, "I nearly went out of my mind, and in the end, I shut myself away. I was going to give that whole fortune away." But the problem was she did not know which organization or mission to give it to. Suddenly, the Lord said to her, "What are you doing?" "I want to know, Lord, who You want me to give this money to." And the Lord said, "Who told you that you had to give up that fortune?" And she said, "But Lord, I thought that is what it meant."

The Lord said to her, "You are not the owner of that fortune; you are the steward. You will do what I tell you to do with it." The amazing thing about dear Lady Ogle was that through prayer she found a brilliant man to supervise that fortune, and over the years she quadrupled and quintupled that fortune and gave away millions—literally. It is very interesting to me, these were two very different cases: one had to give everything away; the other had to use it, but she was still a steward. The British and Foreign Bible Society, the Scripture Gift Mission were more or less kept alive by Lady Ogle's giving. These were great missions having to do with the Word of God. Are you an owner of what you possess or are you a steward?

Priorities

Then there is yet another challenge and that is to get your priorities right. Matthew 6:33 says, "Seek ye first the kingdom of God, and His righteousness; and all these things shall be added unto you." What are all these things? They are clothing, food, and a thousand and one other things. These are the things He says in the previous verse that the Gentiles bother about all the time. I will put it this way: these are the things that the world bothers about and thinks about. What shall we eat? How shall we eat? What shall we be dressed with? How shall we dress? The Lord said, "Get your priorities right. Seek ye first the kingdom of God and His righteousness, and I will take care of all the other things."

I have never found the Lord to be mean. I have never found Him to be stingy in all my life. The Lord is so generous; He loves to give once you have your priorities right. But when your priorities are wrong, you will find everything very difficult. Get your priorities right.

Here is the second shortest verse in the Bible: "Remember Lot's wife." It comes in an amazing chapter about the second coming of the Lord Jesus. In the midst of this chapter, suddenly like a bullet comes this verse: "Remember Lot's wife." Why remember Lot's wife? She was turned into a pillar of salt. What has that got to do with the coming of the Lord? She never got her priorities right. She had a wonderful home in the midst of an unbelievably evil community. She and her husband were famous for their hospitality. Somewhere along the line, the Holy Spirit must have wrestled with Lot's wife to get her priorities clear. But somehow or other she did not rise to it. When the judgment of God fell upon Sodom and Gomorrah, the angels had to carry her out, and then on the way up she kept looking back, and she was turned into a pillar of salt. The church is filled with such pillars of salt, people who have never gotten their priorities clear. They are looking back for the things of the past. Then you become a monument, a gravestone: here lies the body of Lance Lambert, born so and so, died so and so. There are many of Lot's wives in the church. Here is the challenge: Get your priorities right.

Understand the Will of the Lord

There is a fifth challenge. Understand the will of the Lord. Ephesians 5:15–17 says, "Look therefore carefully how ye walk, not as unwise, but as wise; redeeming the time, because the days are evil. Wherefore be ye not foolish, but understand what the will of the Lord is."

The days are evil, increasingly evil, and they will become more and more evil until the anti-Christ appears. Therefore we should not walk unwisely, but wisely, redeeming the time, buying up the opportunity. We should not be foolish, but understand what the will of the Lord is—to be a living sacrifice that ye may prove what is the good, acceptable, well-pleasing and perfect will of God. When you are not a living sacrifice, you are always fearful of the will of God. When you are not under the Lordship of Jesus, when you are an owner and not a steward, when your priorities are wrong, you are always fearful of the will of God. It is as if the Lord is going to damage you; He is going to rob you of joy and life and peace. It is as if when you do the will of the Lord, you will be miserable. It is so stupid. Do you know that your heavenly Father is a father? He does not want to put you into situations that make you miserable, simply for the sake of misery. He loves you, and when He reveals His will, you will always discover in the end, it is good, acceptable, and perfect.

I am old now and waiting for a new body, but I know many very unhappy Christians, and they are without exception believers who do their own will. And I know many Christians who are filled with joy, with life, and even with laughter, and they are all believers who have done the will of God.

1 John 2:15:

"Love not the world, neither the things that are in the world. If any man love the world, the love of the Father is not in him. For all that is in the world, the lust of the flesh, and the lust of the eyes and the vainglory of life is not of the Father, but is of the world. And the world passeth away, and the lust thereof: but he that doeth the will of God abideth forever."

What a wonderful promise! He that does the will of God abides, remains forever. What the Lord does in him is eternal. What the Lord does through him is eternal. Why? He does the will of God. It is as simple at that.

God's Co-workers

That leads me to yet another challenge, and that is the contribution you and I make to the people of God. What do I mean? Look at 1 Corinthians 3:9, 11–15: "For we are God's fellow workers: ye are God's husbandry, God's building … For other foundation can no man lay than that which is laid, which is Jesus Christ. But if any man buildeth on the foundation gold, silver, costly stones, wood, hay, stubble, each man's work shall be made manifest: for the day shall declare it, because it is revealed in fire; and the fire itself shall prove each man's work of what sort it is. If any man's work shall abide which he built thereon, he shall receive a reward. If any man's work shall be burned, he shall suffer loss: but he himself shall be saved; yet so as through fire."

We are God's co-workers. You can either be a co-worker of God or a worker for God. There are two kinds of work—work *for* the Lord and the work *of* the Lord. When you are not a living sacrifice, it is work for the Lord. We are a worker for God. You know the kind of thing: "I have a ministry, I have a work; this is my service. Get behind me, Lord; stand behind me, support me, provide for me, bless me. It is my work and I want You to use it." That is probably putting it a little harshly. When you are a co-worker with God, it is the Lord who calls the shots. You are under government; you do not do what He does not command. It is His work and therefore He provides. When God calls, He always provides in every way. He will provide money on the most mundane level. He will provide anointing on the highest level. When God is the worker, when it is His work, when you are a co-worker together with God under His command, and it is His work, anything can happen.

There are two kinds of material—gold, silver, precious stones, and wood, hay, stubble, and everything is tried by fire. What is going to come through? Certainly not wood, hay and stubble. I remember a number of times going to Imelda Marcos' Coconut Palace in Manila. It was the government's special visitor's guesthouse. I was amazed by it. Everything in it was made out of coconut palm—the wood on the floors, the wood of the banisters, the carpets, the curtains, the lamps, not only the actual lamp, but the lampshade. I could never believe that you could use coconut for so many things. It so amazed me that I walked around in a daze the first time. I kept on saying, "This cannot be coconut." But it was coconut—very beautiful but very flammable.

Many a worker in God's work is building a beautiful building that is flammable. It is ingenious art, brilliant craftsmanship, but wood, hay, and stubble. If what is in you is wood, hay, and stubble, what else can you minister? If you are going to use gold, silver, and precious stones in the building, it has to be in you. Wood, hay, and stubble is worldly. Gold, silver, and precious stone is heavenly as far as heaven is concerned.

These are the challenges. Only a worker who is a living sacrifice can build on the foundation of the Lord Jesus with gold, silver, and precious stone, that which is eternal, that which in the end will be found in the kingdom. The gold and the precious stone will be in the bride and the silver is the means of getting there. What a challenge! What a challenge! We have so little time left to us.

When I was young, which is quite a few years ago, my birthdays seemed to me to be a millennium from each other. I used to bother my mother again and again, "When is my next birthday?"

"You have just had one." "Well, I cannot wait for it." I could not believe that whoever was up there could make it so long until the next birthday. Now my birthdays just fly by. I cannot keep abreast of them. I have to ask the boys, "What age am I now?" It goes so fast. I sometimes wonder if the world is getting faster or is it just me. But the nearer we get to the coming of the Lord, the faster everything will go. You have very little time.

Do not listen to the powers of darkness when they whisper to you, "You are young; enjoy yourself. Enjoy the world; it is there for you. It will not do you any harm; you are young. When you are a little older, you can be more separated from the world."

Then you get married and have children, and the enemy comes and says, "Don't settle these things. You are too busy with your family, and you have too much to do. Bother with your relationships, your family life."

When you arrive at middle-age, you begin to spread out, and the enemy comes and says, "Take it easy. You are middle-aged, and all that fire and fervor are for young people. It is the young people's job and business now; take a little rest. Don't be so one-hundred-percent. It is not necessary; you are middle-aged. Wait until you retire, then you will have time, and you will be able to sit down and sort things out."

Then you get old and you lose your hair, your teeth, and your eyes. And the enemy comes and says, "Don't think the Lord wants you now; you are ready to totter into the grave. You cannot do anything. You have waited too long; you should have settled it when you were young." How clever is the power of darkness! If, today, you hear the Lord's voice, do not harden your heart; this world will destroy you. May God challenge us.

Shall we pray:

Beloved Lord, we ask You not to let us escape. We prayed this at the beginning. Do not let us escape. Corner us, Lord. Have mercy upon us. Save us from the lies of Satan, from his seductive power. Help us to deliberately and coldly, in one sense, present our bodies a living sacrifice. And Lord, we know that You will do the rest. We ask this in the name of our Lord Jesus. Amen.

Other books by Lance Lambert

The Uniqueness of Israel

Woven into the fabric of Jewish existence there is an undeniable uniqueness. There is bitter controversy over the subject of Israel, but time itself will establish the truth about this nation's place in God's plan. For Lance Lambert, the Lord Jesus is the key that unlocks Jewish history He is the key not only to their fall, but also to their restoration. For in spite of the fact that they rejected Him, He has not rejected them.

Till the Day Dawns

"And we have the word of prophecy made more sure; whereunto ye do well that ye take heed, as unto a lamp shining in a dark place, until the day dawn, and the day-star arise in your hearts." (II Peter 1:9).

The word of prophecy was not given that we might merely be comforted but that we would be prepared and made ready. Let us look into the Word of God together, searching out the prophecies, that the Day-Star arise in our hearts until the Day dawns.

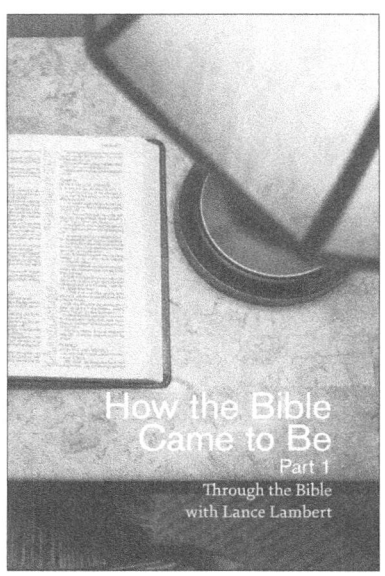

How the Bible Came to Be
Part 1

How is the Bible still as applicable in the 21st century as it was when it was first penned? How did so many authors, with different backgrounds and over thousands of years, write something so perfectly fitting with one another?

Lance Lambert breaks down these, and many other questions in this first volume of his series teaching through the Bible. He lays a firm foundation for going on to study the Word of the living God.

And ye shall seek me, and find me, when ye shall search for me with all your heart. Jeremiah 29:13

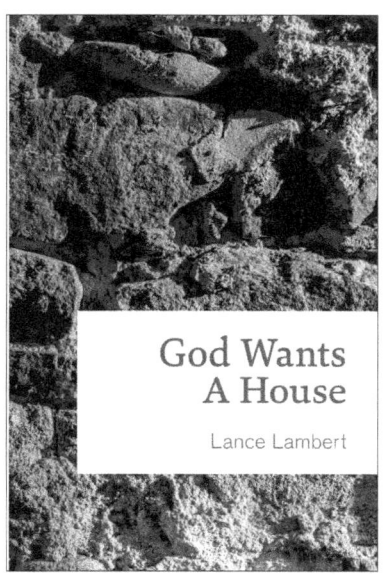

God Wants a House

Where is God at home? Is He at home in Richmond, VA? Is He at home in Washington? Is He at home in Richmond, Surrey? Is He at home in these other places? Where is God at home? There are thousands of living stones, many, many dear believers with real experience of the Lord, but where has the ark come home? Where are the staves being lengthened that God has finally come home? In God Wants a House Lance looks into this desire of the Lord, this desire He has to dwell with His people. What would this dwelling look like? Let's seek the Lord, that we can say with David, "One thing have I asked of Jehovah, that will I seek after: that I may dwell in the house of Jehovah all the days of my life, To behold the beauty of Jehovah, And to inquire in his temple."

www.ingramcontent.com/pod-product-compliance
Lightning Source LLC
Chambersburg PA
CBHW070620050426
42450CB00011B/3091